COLOR CASTING FOR WICCANS

COLOR CASTING FOR WICCANS

Correspondences for More Powerful Spells

SISTER MOON

CITADEL PRESS
KENSINGTON PUBLISHING CORP.
www.kensingtonbooks.com

CITADEL PRESS books are published by

Kensington Publishing Corp.
850 Third Avenue
New York, NY 10022

Copyright © 2001 Sister Moon

All rights reserved. No part of this book may be reproduced in any form or by any means without the prior written consent of the publisher, excepting brief quotes used in reviews.

All Kensington titles, imprints, and distributed lines are available at special quantity discounts for bulk purchases for sales promotions, premiums, fund-raising, educational, or institutional use. Special book excerpts or customized printings can also be created to fit specific needs. For details, write or phone the office of the Kensington special sales manager: Kensington Publishing Corp., 850 Third Avenue, New York, NY 10022, attn: Special Sales Department, phone 1-800-221-2647.

Citadel Press and the Citadel logo are trademarks of Kensington Publishing Corp.

First printing: November 2001

10 9 8 7 6 5 4 3 2 1

Printed in the United States of America

Library of Congress Control Number: 2001094201

ISBN 0-8065-2245-3

This book is dedicated to my sister, Belladonna, the only other person who shares the inheritance of our Grandmother's gift.

The Spell Weaver

Once upon All Hallow's Eve,
A Crone began a spell to weave.
Within a poppet fashioned well,
She whispered words of her spell.
"Gather the Witches for common good,
Link their hands in sisterhood."
One by one, the Witches came,
With a legacy to reclaim.
Enchanted by an unseen force,
Uniting in the Goddess Source.
Gather Sisters for your quest,
Casting magick at your best.
If you question or do not believe,
What that Crone magickally weaved.
Then sideways glance a hastened look,
For other Witches reading this book.
So Mote It Be!

CONTENTS

Acknowledgments   xii
Introduction   xiii
Casting the Circle   xv

1. Spells That Are White   3
   To Discover a Thief • To Purify the Body • To Make the Truth Obvious • To Purify a Home • To Purify a Spell That Has Soured • To Remove Negative Energy • To Banish a Bad-Luck Streak

2. Spells That Are Yellow   13
   To Know Weak From Strong, to Know Right From Wrong • Grandma Dolly's Cure for Chickenpox • To Speed Recovery • To Calm a Willful Child • To Enhance Concentration • To Lose Weight • To Reunite Friends Who Have Quarreled • To Relieve Menstrual Cramps • To Restore Youth; To Look Younger • To Help Retain Learned Information

3. Spells That Are Blue   29
   For Safety During Astral Projection • For Protection From People Who Wish You Harm • For Peace of Mind • To Overcome a Fear of Heights • For Protection During Travel • To Open the Third Eye • To Keep Chaste • To Introduce a New Cat Into Your Home and to Make Feline Members of a Multi-Cat Home Get Along • To Eliminate Panic and Replace It With Tranquility • To Remove All Negative Thoughts and Doubts From a Situation

4. Spells That Are Pink   41
   To Haunt a Man With Love • To Make a Man Confess His Love for You • To Make an Old Lover Return to You • To Bring About a Romantic Relationship • To Become More Beautiful on the Outside

• To Promote Romantic Love • To Stabilize Good Friendships • To Attract and Arouse Male Interest • To Promote Weight Loss • To Ask the Goddess for Blessings

5. **Spells That Are Red**   55

   To Arouse a Man's Passion • For Releasing Anger, Pain, Grief, or Jealousy • To Arouse Your Own Passion • For Courage • To Arouse His Passion • For Endurance During Difficult Times • To Increase Physical Strength • To Light Your Own Fire and Stir Your Female Passion

6. **Spells That Are Orange**   67

   To Solicit a Gray Witch of Yesteryear to Aid You in Any Positive Magickal Endeavor • To Attract a New Love to Your Life • To Attract Customers to a Business • To Receive a Response • To Gain Major Influence Over People • To Attract Good Luck • To Attract a Spouse

7. **Spells That Are Green**   77

   To Bless a Business With Success • To Get a Specific Job • To Become Pregnant • To Sell a House • To Win at Gambling • To Bring Prosperity • To Obtain an Extra $100 • To Get a Loan • To Have Abundance of Wealth in and Around Your Home

8. **Spells That Are Purple**   89

   To Divine Your Future Husband • To Initiate a New Coven • To Divine an Answer • To Divine if Your Lover's Intentions Are True • To Gain Positive Control Over Someone• For Intense Psychic Abilities • To Divine Your Future Mate • To Make a Long-Staying Visitor Want to Leave Your Home • To Receive Prophetic Answers by Way of Your Dreams • To Prevent Someone From Being Accident-Prone • To Communicate With a Specific Person Who Is Deceased

9. **Spells That Are Gold**   103

   To Promote Success in Life • To Bring Success • To Achieve a Personal Goal • To Be Discovered for Your Talents • To Sell a Successful Business • To Extend the Life of Mechanical Devices • To Improve the Memory • To Make Someone Accept a Business

Proposal That Would Be Good for Him or Her and For You • To Find Something That Is Lost • To Obtain Your Daily Goals • To Have Success That Is Blessed by the Gods • To Remove All Obstacles That May Keep Success From Happening

10. Spells That Are Brown   119

    To Keep Your Beloved Male at Home • To Promote Happiness in the Home • For Couples Having Bad Luck in Their Marriage • To Unite in Marriage • To Bring About Marriage • To Solidify a Relationship • To Bring a Lost Pet Back Home • To Keep Your Mate at Home by Your Side • To Obtain a Spouse or Life-Partner • To Return Harmony to the Home After Problems or Upheavals • To Shield Your Partner From a Flirt • To Help Stepsiblings Develop Friendship Bonds • To Encourage a Timely Marriage Proposal

11. Spells That Are Gray   139

    To Counteract the Effects of a Negative Chain Letter • To Repel and Keep Away Negative Energy • To Stop Unwanted Love • For a Divorce • To Return Negativity to Its Source • To Get Rid of a Horrible Neighbor • To Drive Away Someone Who Wishes to Steal Your Lover • To Banish Energy-Stealing Specters and Remove Ghostly Earth Shadows • To Instantly Repel Another • To Remove Obstacles Between You and Your Goal • To Divert Another's Passion For You • To Prevent Slander and Stop Negative Gossip • To Rid a Home of Evil

12. Spells That Are Black   157

    To Put an End to a Lawsuit • To Bind a Negative Energy Forever • To Gain Favor With a Jury or Judge During a Trial • To End Your Poverty • To End an Intense Bad-Luck Streak • To Banish Someone's Obsession With You • To Banish Nightmares • To End Hatred Between Two People • To Win the Favor of the Court or a Jury • To Overcome Guilt and Forgive Yourself • To Dismiss Binds, Known or Unknown, That People Have Put on You • To Make a Negative Person Leave Your Neighborhood

Appendix A: The Sorceress's Sources   173
Appendix B: Table of Magickal Hours of the Day   174
Appendix C: Table of Magickal Hours of the Night   175

ACKNOWLEDGMENTS

I wish to express my undying gratitude to Diane Davis. Thank you for your endless hours of work and for dealing with an impossible Witch. Your efforts and your patience exceed all levels of friendship. At this rate, I am going to have to marry you just to make an honest woman of you. Thank you for taking such good care of me. I love you.

I also wish to thank Bob Berkel, Bruce Bender, and Colette Russen for aiding and abetting me in efforts to produce an organized book of spells.

Last but not least, I would like to extend gratitude to my sister, Belladonna, for sharing her set of spellbooks and for writing the poems that open each chapter. I'd also like to thank my aunt Colleechee for supporting me and sharing her eighty-eight years of wisdom; and finally, thanks to my children for not being embarrassed about having the only mother on the carpool committee who drives a broom.

INTRODUCTION

This book is presented to you with a warning label: Be extremely cautious of what you ask for because chances are, you're going to get it.

Magick is the result of concentrated energy and prayer. When casting magick that involves other people, be aware that there is always a "free will" margin to anticipate. Everyone has been given free will and has the right to either accept or deny on one level or another any spell cast on him or her. Because of this, it's important to keep all magick safe and secret. Any individual who knows of your casting may alter its outcome, an exception being other Witches who may be involved in the spell. There is great power in the secrecy of magick.

Use magick as your last resort, not your first impulse. It is easier to not cast a spell than it is to undo one. Even a badly cast spell is hard to reverse. Think about what you need, what you desire, and how it will affect others. Don't be lazy; first try nonmagickal ways to obtain what you want. If all else fails, then resort to your magick.

The contents of this grimoire are meant to be used by the experienced Witch; however, the format has been simplified to help even a novice achieve success with each spell.

For hundreds of years, our ancestral sisters used color magick in their spellcraft. It is a universal language that all Witches can decipher. Each chapter of this book contains spells that utilize a specific color. For example, if your desire is to draw a new love, look in chapter 4, Spells That Are Pink, for love, or in Spells That Are

Orange, for attraction. If your desire is to obtain a better job, then search in Spells That Are Green, for money, or in Spells That Are Gold, for success. Keep in mind that the color of a spell is based on its *intent,* and not necessarily the actual color of the candles or materials used.

Each of the spells in this book have worked somewhere, somehow, for someone. Some of these spells are over one hundred years old; others are less ancient. It is important to keep in mind that the elements used in each spell can be altered or substituted; however, this is not recommended. In addition, each spell needs to be performed at a specific hour and lunar phase (full moon, Mercury hour; waning moon, Saturn hour, for example). Appendixes B and C include tables of the magickal hours of the day and night to aid you in identifying the precise time to perform your spell.

Remember to cast a circle and incorporate the help of the quadrants and the Goddess and God before casting any spell. Cleanse your area and your altar well and have all tools ready at your fingertips.

It is recommended that your incenses and oils be purchased from occult stores or, if they are homemade, be sure you allow the ingredients to meld together for no less than one moon cycle. All herbs and botanicals should be fresh and no more than one season old. Any candles you use should be solid colors and should be fragrance free. See Appendix A for the address of an occult supplier that carries many of the ingredients for the spells in this book.

The rest is up to you, dear Witch. With the approval of the Goddess and God, a pure heart, and the intention to harm none, your outcome will be magick!

Blessed Be!

CASTING THE CIRCLE

Light the Unity candle.
Place three pinches of salt into the ritual water. Say:

I cleanse thee, Spirit of Salt and Spirit of Water. I cast out all impurities that lie within thee. This is my will, So Mote It Be.

Working clockwise, sprinkle the perimeter of the circle with the salt water.

Face East, and draw a pentagram in the air with your athame, starting at the top point. Say:

Raphael: I call upon the powers of the East. May the air lift me so my mind will feast.

Face South and make the sign of the pentagram with your athame. Say:

Michael: I call upon the powers of the South. May the fire of free will never burn out.

Face West and make the sign of the pentagram with your athame. Say:

Gabriel: I call upon the powers of the West. May the water of emotion join my quest.

Face North and make the sign of the pentagram with your athame. Say:

> Uriel: I call upon the powers of the North. May the earth be
> my body from this day forth. So Mote It Be.

Light the God candle on the left from the Unity Candle and say:

> I call upon God, Creator of Man. I welcome thee to
> empower this magick circle.

Light the Goddess candle on the right from the Unity Candle and say:

> I call upon Goddess, Creator of Woman. I welcome thee to
> empower this magick circle.

To Release the Circle

Face West, and, with the athame, draw a sign of the pentagram in the air, starting at the bottom left of the star. Say:

> To the North, South, East, and West,
> With gratitude and praise and so be blessed.

Extinguish the God candle and then the Goddess candle and say:

> To the mighty God and the Goddess that be,
> With gratitude and praise, So Mote It Be.

Hold the Unity Candle in your hands and say:

> This candle now shines of one.
> My journey has now begun.
> This circle is now open,
> But forever, unbroken.
> So Mote It Be.

Extinguish the Unity Candle.

COLOR CASTING FOR WICCANS

1

SPELLS THAT ARE *White*

> To catch the rain upon the tongue,
> Transforms the mind to days of young.
> Drink in the moonlight to again endure,
> A time of when the heart was pure.
> —Belladonna

The color white represents magick involving the higher self, purity of heart, cleansing, truth seeking, sacred paths, absolution, removing unwanted energy, and forgiveness.

To Discover a Thief

Frost Bite

TIME   Waning Saturday, Mercury hour.

TOOLS   One white candle, Magick oil, a piece of white string about twenty-four inches long, Four Thieves powder, Lily of the Valley incense, and four small mirrors.

INSTRUCTIONS   Ask the God to be with you during this spell. Anoint the white candle with the Magick oil. Place the candle in the center of your working area. Make a large circle around the candle with the white string. Sprinkle a heavy layer of Four Thieves Powder within the circle. Light the candle and the incense. Place the small mirrors in the four directions of the circle and use them to reflect the powder. Recite the incantation. The thief's initials or face will be shown in the powder, or the seeker will have a dream that reveals the thief's identity. All will be told within three nights of the casting.

INCANTATION

Like roaches that creep around the night,
Crawl through powder with a name to write.
A thief has stolen from this Witch,
Reveal the name as if a snitch.
Draw a sign, show me a face,
The search for truth begins to chase.
Blackened halls and shadows of frost,
Forever to chase this soul of lost.
Reveal it all within this powder,
Aid this Witch with magickal power.
Truth be known in all that I seek,
Give to me now the name of my thief.
So Mote It Be.

To Purify the Body

The Body Bag

TIME   Hare Moon, Sun hour.

TOOLS   Three white candles, Moonlight oil, Amulet incense, a bath steeper or muslin bag, star anise, bay leaf, lemon, chamomile, and Exodus bath salts.

INSTRUCTIONS   In the bathroom (or wherever you bathe) draw a bath. Anoint the three candles with Moonlight oil. Light the candles and place them around the bathtub; light the incense. Place the anise, bay leaf, lemon, and chamomile in the bath steeper. Place seven tablespoons of Exodus bath salts directly into your bath. By the light of the three candles, place the bath steeper into the bath with you and relax. Recite the incantation. Allow all of the bathwater to drain from the tub before you get out.

INCANTATION

Brew of Exodus, I conjure thee,
Liberate the darkness within me.
I offer chamomile, lemon, and leaf of bay,
To banish, release, and take away.
Star anise is added for purity,
Steeped beneath for certainty.
Drain the dimness, restore the light,
Cleanse me like the Goddess white.
Purge this body to be unstained,
Flush the darkness down the drain.
My body is pure, my body is free,
This is my will, So Mote It Be.

TO MAKE THE TRUTH OBVIOUS

Not a Shadow of a Doubt

TIME   Waning Saturday, Saturn hour.

TOOLS   One large white candle, Lily of the Valley oil, Uncrossing incense, a white rose with green leaves on it in a vase, white parchment, Dove's Blood ink (or any red ink), and tape.

INSTRUCTIONS   Anoint the candle with Lily of the Valley oil. Light the candle and the incense. Pull three green leaves from the white rose. Pass the white rose three times over the incense in a widdershins direction. Place the rose in a vase of cold water. Divide the parchment into three sections with your red ink. On one third, write: "The situation is true to how it is seen." On the second section, write: "The situation is false to how it is seen." On the last section, write: "The situation is gray." (This would mean there is half-true and half-false information involved.) Tape one leaf on each third of the parchment. Recite the incantation. Place the parchment under the vase with the rose. After the rose has been dead for three days, look at the leaves taped to the parchment. The greenest, most alive-looking leaf will reveal the truth about the situation. If the answer is true, then your option to go for it would be best. If the answer is false, then you must abandon your course. If the answer is gray, redirect your course of action to make it more suitable for the situation. No matter what is revealed, the situation will change according to the truth.

INCANTATION

> Virgin rose that Goddess creates,
> Reveal to me the perfect fate.
> I call upon Your power so wise,
> Disclose truth, grays, or lies.
> Truth be told upon the leaf,
> I embrace reply with belief.
> Where life and greenery still abound,
> My best passage will be found.
> Goddess of the earthly garden,
> Suspicion lurks without pardon.
> Silence be broken with a shout,
> Truths reveal without shadow of doubt.
> So Mote It Be.

To Purify a Home

Four Corners

TIME   Hare Moon, Sun hour.

TOOLS   Four white candles, House Blessing oil, Drive Away Evil incense, an earthen bowl or mortar and pestle, chamomile, fennel, lavender, rosemary, and four red mojos.

INSTRUCTIONS   Anoint the four white candles with House Blessing oil. Set the four white candles at the cardinal points of the circle

Blend the herbs into powder

to represent the four corners or quadrants. Light the candles and the incense. In an earthen bowl, blend and grind the herbs into a powder. Add four drops of House Blessing oil to the mixture. Separate the herbs into the four mojos. Recite the incantation and suffumigate the mojos by passing them through the incense smoke. Place each mojo in an east, south, west, or north corner of your home. On the next March 20, bury the mojos and make new ones for the next year.

INCANTATION

> *Magickal mixture and blessings be,*
> *Towers Four I call to thee.*
> *Bless this home and all who dwell,*
> *Cleanse each space within the shell.*
> *Keep the darkness all at bay,*
> *Brighten and cleanse in every way.*
> *This house be pure, this home be white,*
> *Keep us safe from day to night.*
> *So Mote It Be.*

TO PURIFY A SPELL THAT HAS SOURED

Knights in White Satin

TIME   Full Moon, Moon hour.

TOOLS   One large white candle, Criss-Cross oil, Moonlight incense, a black marker, a piece of white parchment, four strips of white satin, four knights (pentacles, wands, swords, and cups) from any tarot deck, and a small white feather.

INSTRUCTIONS   Anoint the candle with Criss-Cross oil. Light the candle and the incense. Using the black marker, on the white parchment write down the name of the spell that has gone sour. On the first strip of satin, write: EAST: Purify thee; on the second: SOUTH:

Purify thee; on the third: WEST: Purify thee; and on the last: NORTH: Purify thee. Place the tarot knights on the parchment in a crosslike shape. Place one strip over each of the knights. Place the white feather in the center of the cross. For the next twenty-eight days, recite the incantation and sweep the feather over one knight, alternating knights every day. At the end of the twenty-eight days, bury the four strips of satin and the parchment (but not the cards) near a fruit-bearing tree.

INCANTATION

> *Cleanse the spell of which I cast,*
> *Purify it now from beginning to last.*
> *I invoke the aid of all Four Towers,*
> *Knights be cleansed with virgin power.*
> *So Mote It Be.*

TO REMOVE NEGATIVE ENERGY

Eclipsing of Negative Energies

TIME   Waning Saturday, Sun hour.

TOOLS   One white candle, Jinx Removing oil, Uncrossing incense, an athame, consecrated or holy water, a hematite, Lady Luck oil, Good Luck incense, a red mojo, and as many Witches as you can get to help in the casting (one Witch will be the acting High Priestess).

INSTRUCTIONS   Anoint the white candle with Jinx Removing oil. Light the candle and the Uncrossing incense.

Have the victim of the negative energy stand in the center of the circle of Witches. With the athame, cut the cords and threads of negativity that are attached to the person while the High Priestess recites the first incantation several times; the participating Witches will echo her. Sprinkle a magick circle around the victim with the consecrated water while the High Priestess recites the second incantation several times with the other Witches repeating after her. As the High Priestess is reciting the second incantation, she must anoint the pulse points or the feet and head of the victim with the consecrated water.

The High Priestess passes the hematite widdershins through the incense smoke while reciting the third incantation several times, the other Witches repeating it after her. Feel the negative energy release.

When the energy is completely gone, it is time to fill the person with white energy and a dash of good luck. Light the Good Luck incense. The High Priestess passes the hematite stone deosil through the incense smoke while reciting the fourth incantation, all Witches repeating after her.

Anoint the person's third eye with the Lady Luck oil. All Witches should visualize the person filling up with white light starting from her feet and ending with the crown chakra.

The High Priestess recites the fifth incantation one time, repeated by the Witches.

The hematite should be placed into the red mojo and given to the subject of the ritual.

The negative energy is completely released and there should be significant changes by the next full moon.

INCANTATION 1

We cut the cord with the mighty sword.

INCANTATION 2

Negative release now marked with peace.

INCANTATION 3

Release the black and all attack.

INCANTATION 4

Fill with white the Holy Light.

INCANTATION 5

Forever white light is now within,
Never to darken and never to dim.
Shining bright for all to see,
This is our will, So Mote It Be!

To Banish a Bad-Luck Streak

The Banishing Bath

TIME   Waxing Monday, Moon hour.

TOOLS   Two large white candles, Banishing oil, Uncrossing incense, Devil's shoestring, lemon juice, pepper, copal, sage, and two tablespoons of sea salt.

INSTRUCTIONS   Anoint the two white candles with Banishing oil. Light the candles and the incense. To a bathtub filled with very warm water, add the herbs and the sea salt, and stir. After the water has become still, add two drops of Banishing oil. Get in the bathtub.

After meditating on releasing the bad luck, let the herbs soak into your body. Visualize a white light entering the water. See the darkness coming out of your skin. Notice the white light illuminating your body.

Recite the incantation.

(When you drain the bath, be sure to place a screen or piece of muslin over the drain to catch the used herbs so they will not plug up the drain.)

INCANTATION

Boil the devil in purifying bath,
When evil abounds your body and path.
Lemon, pepper, copal, and sage,
Removes the demons and the rage.
Add two spoons of Dead Sea salt,
To make the darkness come to a halt.
Banishing oil when the water is still,
Keep it warm without a chill.
Third eye open to see the light,
Fill the soul on a moonlit night.
Restore good luck and all be well,
Bad luck gone and forever dispelled.
So Mote It Be.

2

SPELLS THAT ARE *Yellow*

> Reclaim the sun that warms the soul,
> Radiant daystar, take control!
> Heal the body, mind, and heart,
> Convert to light what once was dark.
> —Belladonna

The color yellow represents magick involving healing, health matters, intelligence, happiness, state of mind, confidence, and self-esteem.

To Know Weak From Strong, To Know Right From Wrong

Time Hare Moon, Moon hour.

Tools One large yellow candle, a small white votive candle, Lemon Drops oil, Positive Attitude incense, and a crystal ball.

INSTRUCTIONS Anoint the yellow candle and the white votive candle with Lemon Drops oil. Light the candles and the incense. Place the white votive candle behind the crystal ball so you can see the flame when you look through the crystal. Place the yellow candle behind the burning incense and off to the left of the crystal. Recite the incantation and gaze into the crystal. If you see a definite blue image in the crystal, then do nothing to help this individual. If you see any color other than blue, then you may assist this person with magick. If you see any image of an animal, then you must only help them monetarily. If the crystal ball grows dark, ask at another time.

INCANTATION

Eye of Tiger burning the amber,
I ask the question for you to answer.
A person is in need of divine aid,
Do I help or do I remain?
Reveal to me for right or wrong,
Are they weak or are they strong?
If crystal globe contains the blue,
I shall not help if this is true.
Any other color that I shall see,
I shall assist them magickally.
If an animal is in the midst,
Gold and silver I shall insist.
But if the globe grows dark with gray,
I shall wait and ask another day.
So Mote It Be.

GRANDMA DOLLY'S CURE FOR CHICKENPOX

TIME Any day, Sun hour.

TOOLS One yellow candle, Healing oil, High Meadows incense, burdock leaves, echinacea, chamomile, and green tea.

Spells That Are Yellow

A potion for healing

INSTRUCTIONS   Anoint the candle with Healing oil. Light the candle and the incense. Combine burdock leaves, echinacea, and chamomile in a tea steeper. Boil in an earthen pot for twenty minutes. Combine with green tea. Recite the incantation. Serve five times during the day and five times after dark for ten consecutive days.

INCANTATION

> *Blend a potion of burdock leaves,*
> *Echinacea, chamomile in green teas.*
> *Drink for total of ten days to cleanse,*

The virus of the chickens and hens.
Five times day, five times night,
Makes the chicken leave the fight.
Rest the child till virus be gone,
Spots remove with each new dawn.
So Mote It Be.

To Speed Recovery

The Healing Flame

TIME   Waxing Sunday or Monday, Mars hour.

TOOLS   A wick, a metal washer, a small piece of clay, a glass container, a pencil, beeswax (available at craft stores), a double boiler, eucalyptus leaves, green tea, three orange seeds, a yellow crayon, Healing oil, and sliced lemon rind.

INSTRUCTIONS   Tie one end of the wick to the washer. Put a pinch of clay in the bottom of the container and stick the washer securely in the clay. Tie the wick that hangs outside of the container to the pencil and roll it up. Rest the pencil across the container, pulling the wick tight.

Over low heat, melt the wax in the double boiler; meanwhile, grind up the eucalyptus, green tea, and orange seeds. When the wax is completely melted, add the yellow crayon, ten drops of the Healing oil, the sliced lemon rind, and the tea mixture. Recite the incantation. Pour the wax into the glass container. After the candle has hardened, cut off the excess wick. Use the candle whenever you are sick or give it to someone else to help them have a speedy recovery.

INCANTATION

Healing candle, healing flame,
Release the sickness and the pain.

> *Cleanse the body and restore the health,*
> *Complete vitality of Goddess wealth.*
> *So Mote It Be.*

To Calm a Willful Child

Calming the Spirit

TIME   Waning Saturday, Saturn hour.

TOOLS   One blue candle, Carnation oil, Peace incense, and Rose oil.

INSTRUCTIONS   Anoint the candle with Carnation oil. Light the candle and the incense. Mix some Carnation oil with the Rose oil in a container and pray for the willful child to calm herself. Pass the oil mixture through the incense. Ask for the healing angels to give you the divine touch. (It's helpful to have soothing music playing in the background.) Have the child lay her head on your lap. Anoint her temple area with the oil. As you massage the temples, work your fingers over the forehead until she closes her eyes. This is the first sign that the healing angels have given you the divine touch. As the child is relaxing, gently stroke the back of the neck and the collarbone area. Work your way down the arms and on to the hands. Place a drop of the oil behind the ears and massage them. Then recite the incantation several times while the child is completely relaxed.

INCANTATION

> *Blessings my child,*
> *Calm and relaxed.*
> *Listen to my heart,*
> *And feel my love.*
> *So Mote It Be.*

To Enhance Concentration

Mind the Mirror

TIME   Waxing Wednesday, Mercury hour.

TOOLS   One yellow candle, Memory oil, Concentration incense, a small round mirror, a small glass jar, and a piece of yellow cloth.

Mental image

INSTRUCTIONS   Anoint the candle with Memory oil. Take the candle, incense, mirror, and jar with you to a body of water and light them. Call upon the Goddess and ask Her to come to you. When you feel Her presence, state your need. Ask for knowledge and memory. Ask the Goddess to keep you focused and absorbed in your learning process. When you feel Her approval, go to the water and wash your mirror. Gather some of the water in the jar. Hold the mirror to reflect Her presence. Recite the incantation. Keep the mirror covered with the yellow cloth when not studying. When you need to study for a test or need extra powers of concentration, uncover the mirror and anoint your forehead with water from the jar.

INCANTATION

> *Gracious Lady of the Waxing Light,*
> *Expand my knowledge and mental sight.*
> *I feel Your presence when You are near,*
> *Imprint Your image upon rounded mirror.*
> *Bless this water with retention,*
> *Lift my mind to ascension.*
> *Give to me the knowledge I ask,*
> *So I may conquer this mental task.*
> *So Mote It Be.*

To Lose Weight

A-B-C

TIME   The first day after the Full Moon, Venus hour. The days that follow are in the waning phase and should be performed during the Venus hour.

TOOLS   One pink candle, Lovely oil, Venus incense, two cups of apple juice, a cup of cherries, and a banana.

INSTRUCTIONS   Anoint the pink candle with Lovely oil. Light the candle and the incense. Pray to the Goddess that your body release all its impurities and become healthier, stronger, slimmer, and lighter. Combine the two cups of apple juice, one cup of cherries, and one ripe banana in a blender; add about five ice cubes and blend. This potion replaces two meals per day; eat sensibly for the third meal. Recite the incantation before drinking this potion. This spell works best if you drink this mixture twice a day at the Venus hours and eat sensibly.

INCANTATION

> *I ask for radiant health,*
> *May this potion be the key.*
> *I ask for strength and power,*
> *With the potion of A-B-C.*
> *I ask for a slimmer body,*
> *May this potion be the key.*
> *I ask to reduce my size,*
> *With the potion of A-B-C.*
> *I ask for beauty and joy,*
> *May this potion be the key.*
> *I ask impurities to wane,*
> *With the potion of A-B-C.*
> *This is my will,*
> *So Mote It Be.*

TO REUNITE FRIENDS WHO HAVE QUARRELED

Happy Two-Gether

TIME   Waxing Thursday, Mercury hour.

TOOLS   One yellow candle, Friendship oil, Springtime incense, sweetpea herb, a gold ring, one white feather, and three peacock rocks.

Gold band, peacock rocks, and a feather

INSTRUCTIONS   Anoint the candle with Friendship oil. Light the candle and the incense. Send telepathic messages to your friend asking to heal the rift between you and restore the friendship. When you feel the negative energy lift, place the sweetpea herb inside the gold ring. Sweep the feather deosil around the peacock rocks three times. Recite the incantation. Leave the spell setup undisturbed. Send a telepathic message each day to your friend as you light the candle. When positive communication is reestablished between you and your friend, bury the sweetpea in the ground. Release the white feather to the wind. Give your friend one of the stones, retain one for yourself and throw the other stone into a body of water.

INCANTATION

> *Friends together,*
> *Friends alone.*
> *Sweetpea, feather,*
> *Peacock stones.*
> *Quarrel be done,*
> *Restore and repair.*
> *Days of fun,*
> *Again we share.*
> *So Mote It Be.*

TO RELIEVE MENSTRUAL CRAMPS

The Blood Bath

TIME   First and fourth day of the period.

TOOLS   A pinch of each of the following: chamomile, cramp bark, dong quai (only if grown in the same country in which you live), red raspberry, one large yellow candle, Goddess oil, Sunshine incense, Crystal Bell bath salts, a washcloth, and gingerroot.

INSTRUCTIONS   Brew at least four cups of tea made from the chamomile, cramp bark, dong quai, and red raspberry. Anoint the candle with the Goddess oil. Light the candle and the incense and bring all items with you to the bathroom. Draw a warm bath and add Crystal Bell bath salts. With a washcloth, make a compress with the gingerroot. Place the compress on your tummy. Recite the incantation over the brew. Drink two cups of the brewed tea and pour two cups of the remaining tea over the compress. Keep the bathwater warm and sit back and relax. Dim all of the lights except for the light of the yellow candle.

Incantation

> *Goddess of Joy, God of Wrath,*
> *Heal my body in the Blood Bath.*
> *I ask the Angels to ease the pain,*
> *Release the tension and the strain.*
> *Heal my organs so they won't seize,*
> *Calm the muscles so the pain will ease.*
> *I accept my privilege of the female form,*
> *Restore the comfort and make me warm.*
> *Raspberry, chamomile, dong quai, and bark,*
> *Brewed with magick and drunk in the dark.*
> *Root of ginger will absorb the flame,*
> *And ease the cramp of the bloody dame.*
> *So Mote It Be.*

A magickal bath to relieve the pain of menstrual cramps

To Restore Youth; To Look Younger

Fountain of Youth

TIME   Hare Moon, Sun Hour.

TOOLS   One yellow candle, Springtime oil, Dancing Faeries incense, a teaspoon of rosemary, a pinch of vervain, a cup of water obtained from a fountain that has one or more mermaids in it (the mermaids may be real or made of a material), and three tablespoons of Mermaid's Song bath salts.

INSTRUCTIONS   Anoint the candle with Springtime oil. Light the candle and the incense. Draw a warm bath. Place the rosemary and the vervain in the cup of fountain water. Place the Mermaid's Song bath salts in the bathwater. Get into the warm bath and slowly pour the cup of water over your body. Recite the incantation. Allow the potion to sink into your body. Feel the years erase from your life. Allow yourself to feel your strength restore itself in your body. Feel the rejuvenation of a younger time come over you. (You may repeat this spell as many as four times a year.)

INCANTATION

> *Mermaids of the endless flow,*
> *Erase the years that outward show.*
> *Restore the child of youthful blood,*
> *Energy surge with reckless flood.*
> *Children of the infinite sea,*
> *Come right now and play with me.*
> *Turn back time to a happier youth,*
> *Give to me a younger truth.*
> *So Mote It Be.*

Representations of mermaids are often used in spells dealing with love, beauty, and loneliness.

To Help Retain Learned Information

The Thinking Cap

TIME   Waxing Wednesday, Mercury hour.

TOOLS   One yellow candle, Memory oil, Concentration incense, a handful of fresh spearmint, a handful of dried rosemary, and an earthen bowl.

INSTRUCTIONS   Anoint the candle with Memory oil. Light the candle and the incense. Place the fresh spearmint and the dried rosemary in the earthen bowl. Recite the incantation. Visualize intense energy entering the mixture. Rub a handful of mixture on the person

A great spell to use on students of all ages

who needs to retain knowledge. Rub it across the forehead, on the back of the head, neck, and around the ears. (It smells great!) Recite the incantation two more times after you have rubbed the mixture on. Automatic retention of information will be delivered that day. (Note: This spell can be used anytime after it has been empowered.)

INCANTATION

Spirit of Spearmint,
Rose of rosemary.
Power of scent,
Retain and carry.
Mind will learn,
Knowledge be power,
Flame will burn,
This mercury hour.
So Mote It Be.

3

SPELLS THAT ARE *Blue*

> Tranquil moments of summer's rain,
> Eases the mind of fear and pain.
> Dragons of blue will never forget,
> Who it is they need to protect.
> —Belladonna

The color blue represents magick involving protection, safety, peacefulness, tranquility, protection during astral projection, reassurance, and creative energies.

FOR SAFETY DURING ASTRAL PROJECTION

Witch's Flying Ointment

TIME   Hare Moon, Sun hour.

TOOLS   One blue candle, Astral Projection oil, Astral Projection incense, a pinch of dittany of Crete, mugwort, poplar, vegetable lard, a mortar and pestle, and an earthen bowl.

INSTRUCTIONS   Anoint the candle with Projection oil. Light the candle and the incense. Grind the dittany of Crete, mugwort, and poplar with the mortar and pestle until they are powdered. Combine the powdered herbs and the vegetable lard in an earthen bowl. Add a dash of Astral Projection oil and stir well. Recite the incantation. Rub the mixture on the third eye and on the pulse points of the body before engaging in astral projection.

INCANTATION

> *Fly by day, fly by night,*
> *Fly by broom, fly by kite.*
> *Velvet blue surround the brew,*
> *Keep me safe in all I do.*
> *Round and round the cream is stirred,*
> *Fly me high and away like a bird.*
> *Body safe and body stay,*
> *Protect from evil while away.*
> *The soul to see and know the flight,*
> *Keep the cord safe in sight.*
> *Magick potion of flying blue,*
> *Keep me safe in all I do.*
> *So Mote It Be.*

For Protection From People Who Wish You Harm

Bean, Basil, and Broom

TIME   Waning Tuesday, Saturn hour.

TOOLS   Three blue candles, Lotus oil, Protection incense, nine straws from a Witch's broom, twenty-seven navy beans, three pinches of basil and one red mojo.

INSTRUCTIONS   Anoint the candles with Lotus oil. Light the candles and the incense. Visualize a thick, blue aura around yourself,

Broom to fly by night

protecting you from any harm. Break the straws from the broom into small pieces. Place the straw, beans, and basil into the red mojo. Pass the mojo through the incense smoke while reciting the incantation.

Keep the mojo near you at all times. Light the blue candles and recite the incantation whenever you feel danger.

INCANTATION

> *Bean, basil, and broom,*
> *My enemies are entombed.*
> *They're powerless and weak,*
> *They have no voice to speak.*
> *I am safe and strong,*
> *From those who wish me wrong.*
> *Protection in the sack,*
> *From enemy attack.*
> *So Mote It Be.*

For Peace of Mind

The Morning Map

TIME   Waning Monday, Moon hour of daytime only.

TOOLS   One blue candle, Moon oil, Tranquility incense, a blue ink pen, blue parchment, and seven green olives.

INSTRUCTIONS   Perform this spell outside under a willow tree. Anoint the candle with Moon oil. Light the candle and the incense. With the blue pen and blue parchment, list all of the problems that bother you. Write them in detail and number them. Draw a circle on the parchment around the problems you listed. Visualize all of the problems being erased from the list one by one. With your eyes closed, eat the seven green olives and recite the incantation. Bury the parchment under the willow tree and rest assured that the problems will be resolved in a timely manner. Peace will envelop you.

INCANTATION

> *I ask for all to feel the peace,*
> *Relax, resolve, repose, release.*
> *Morning map bears the score,*
> *Relax, resolve, there is no more.*
> *Seven olives ingest by moon,*
> *Relax, resolve, repose, retune.*
> *Willow conquer, trouble decease,*
> *Relax, resolve, repose, peace.*
> *So Mote It Be.*

TO OVERCOME A FEAR OF HEIGHTS

On the Wings of a Bird

TIME   Waxing Tuesday, Mars hour.

TOOLS   One blue candle, Tranquility oil, Dove's Flight incense, one piece of straw, one star anise, a red mojo, five blades of grass, and consecrated water.

INSTRUCTIONS   Anoint the candle with Tranquility oil. Light the candle and the incense. Wrap the straw around the star anise. Visualize the color blue. Place it in the red mojo. Visualize blue wings. Place the five blades of grass in the mojo. Visualize a white dove. Seal the mojo. Anoint it with consecrated water. Pass the mojo deosil through the incense smoke. Recite the incantation. Carry the mojo with you when you know that you will need to overcome the fear of heights.

INCANTATION

> *Angels of the Wind,*
> *And Angels of the Sea.*
> *I call upon discipline,*

*For all my fears to flee.
Angels of the Flame,
Shield me from descention.
This amulet acclaim,
Bounty your protection.
Angels of Earthen love,
I ask to hear you sing.
Convert me to a white dove,
And carry me on your wings.
So Mote It Be.*

Peace, protection, and safety

For Protection During Travel

The Rolling Stones

TIME Full Moon, Saturn hour.

TOOLS One blue candle, Protection oil, Dove's Flight incense, a piece of blue satin, an aquamarine, a tonka bean, a protection rune, and a red mojo.

INSTRUCTIONS Anoint the candle with Protection oil. Light the candle and the incense. Create a pouch out of the blue satin and place the stone, bean, and rune inside of the material; sew it shut. Visualize a blue aura blazing from the pouch. Toss the pouch high into the air while reciting the incantation. Place the pouch in the red mojo and carry it with you during travel.

INCANTATION

> *Rolling stones,*
> *Protecting zone.*
> *Blue holds three,*
> *So Mote It Be.*

To Open the Third Eye

20/20/20 Vision

TIME Full Moon, Moon hour.

TIME A scrying mirror, one blue candle, Blue Gypsy oil, and Blue Moon incense.

INSTRUCTIONS It is important to be calm and relaxed before starting this spell. The room should be dark; the only light will be the candle.

Set the mirror on a table and sit comfortably with the scrying mirror flat on the table directly before you, reflecting surface up.

Anoint the candle with Blue Gypsy oil. Light the candle and the incense. Pray to the Goddess and God to open your third eye and visualize it opening. Recite the incantation and gaze upon the mirror. You will actually see a third eye appear and open between your eyebrows. At this point, rest assured that your psychic channel is opened.

INCANTATION

Open the eye so I may see,
Visions of the mysteries.
Gypsy eye will now expose,
Within the glass it will glow.
By smoke and flame of Moon hour,
I receive the gift of the power.
Grant this vision without fear,
As I shine the magickal mirror.
So Mote It Be.

TO KEEP CHASTE

Leper Erised

TIME   Waning Friday, Mars hour.

TOOLS   One blue candle, Lavender Blue oil, Witching Well incense, a blue pen, a piece of white parchment, a mirror, and two white roses.

INSTRUCTIONS   Anoint the candle with Lavender Blue oil. Light the candle and the incense.

With the pen, write the words *leper erised* on the white parchment. Place the parchment against the mirror so the words are reflected in it.

Place the two white roses on the threshold of a church. Recite the incantation over the threshold and leave the roses there.

Anytime that you feel an overwhelming urge to have sex, relight the blue candle, read the words in the mirror, and take a cold shower.

INCANTATION

> *Reflector repel leper,*
> *Erised reverse desire.*
> *Lust be gone forever,*
> *Chastity quench fire.*
> *Wolves pursue daughters,*
> *Daughters are chaste.*
> *Ice cool with water,*
> *All desires erased.*
> *So Mote It Be.*

TO INTRODUCE A NEW CAT INTO YOUR HOME AND TO MAKE FELINE MEMBERS OF A MULTI-CAT HOME GET ALONG

Calming the Kittens

TIME   Waning Saturday, Venus hour.

TOOLS   One blue candle for each cat in the home, Tranquility oil, Blue Gypsy incense, one-quarter teaspoon of tobacco, three tablespoons of catnip, one bird's feather (naturally fallen from a bird, not removed), naturally removed hairs from each cat (stroking from head to tail), and one red flannel mojo.

INSTRUCTIONS   Anoint each candle with Tranquility oil. Light the candles and the incense. Place the herbs, feather, and cat hairs into the mojo. Before you force an introduction of the cats, rub the mojo on each cat separately and allow the cats to smell the mojo. Recite the incantation over each cat. If using this spell to introduce a new cat, repeat rubbing each cat with the mojo every day for one week before the new cat is to assume residence.

INCANTATION

Light each candle for each cat,
Stroke the fur front to back.
In the mojo they will meld,
With tobacco, feather, and catnip held.
Say these words with each stroke,
"Familiars be friends and friends be blokes."
Each day passing they'll learn to play,
Eat and purr from night to day.
So Mote It Be.

Potion to prevent cat attacks

To Eliminate Panic and Replace It With Tranquility

Burrito Baby

TIME   Waning Tuesday, Sun hour.

TOOLS   One blue candle, Peace oil, Tranquility incense, a soft blue cotton material that measures 70 inches by 70 inches or a blanket that is already made and altered to fit these dimensions, and enough blue satin binding to go the circumference of the blanket. Thermal-type materials that are one hundred percent cotton work best.

INSTRUCTIONS   Anoint the candle with Peace oil. Light the candle and the incense. Suffumigate the blanket in the incense seven times. Anoint the satin binding with the oil. Recite the incantation. Wrap yourself in the blanket any time you feel the onset of panic or anxiety.

INCANTATION

> *Woven threads of mystic blue,*
> *Tranquility expels its calming hue.*
> *Release the burdens of this world,*
> *Safe within this womb I'm curled.*
> *Goddess bestow your infinite grace,*
> *Now within this protected place.*
> *Securely wrapped in Your loving arms,*
> *Never to worry of danger or harm.*
> *God will battle all the woes,*
> *No longer will I have the foes.*
> *For I am safe and all is at peace,*
> *All is perfect and time will cease.*
> *So Mote It Be.*

TO REMOVE ALL NEGATIVE THOUGHTS AND DOUBTS FROM A SITUATION

Doubting Thomas

TIME Waning Wednesday, Sun hour.

TOOLS One blue candle, one white candle, Purity oil, Witching Well incense, three pinches of doggrass, two pinches of yellow dock, one pinch of khus-khus, and a smidgen of dandelion, earthen bowl or mortar and pestle.

INSTRUCTIONS Anoint both candles with Purity oil. Light the candles and the incense. Mix all herbal ingredients together in an earthen bowl or with a mortar and pestle. Suffumigate the herbs in the incense. Add three drops of Purity oil to the mixture. Recite the incantation. Sprinkle the mixture in the four corners of the room in which you have negative thoughts or doubts. This spell will remove confusion and allow positive energy to flow through.

INCANTATION

> *Dandelion for purity in thought,*
> *A clearer mind now is sought.*
> *Add yellow dock and khus-khus,*
> *Keep me close to simple truth.*
> *Purity oil and doggrass,*
> *Keeps me on a narrow path.*
> *No more doubt or confusion,*
> *As I conjure this infusion.*
> *There is no doubt,*
> *There is no fear.*
> *I now believe,*
> *The Angels are here.*
> *No longer alone,*
> *My mind is free.*
> *No longer discouraged,*
> *So Mote It Be.*

4

SPELLS THAT ARE *Pink*

Goddess embrace the mortal mind,
Cradle the child that you find.
Encourage the love that dares to grow,
Beneath the stars and within the soul.
—Belladonna

The color pink represents magick involving true love, romance, healing emotional issues, beauty, caring, nurturing, maturity, unconditional love, friendship, and fantasies.

To Haunt a Man With Love

The Shell Spell

TIME   Hare Moon, Venus hour.

TOOLS   One pink candle, Kitten Love oil, Pink Musk incense, and one beautiful seashell. (Shells are one of the few items that hold energy through hundreds of years. Their energy is all feminine. It is one of the most natural ways to haunt someone without the person even knowing it.)

INSTRUCTIONS   Anoint the candle with Kitten Love oil. For fourteen consecutive days, light the candle and the incense and suffumigate the shell with the incense smoke as you say the incantation. Do this at the Venus hour each time. Never reveal to anyone what the shell means.

Ask the person to keep the shell near his or her bed at all times. The person will be constantly haunted by thoughts of you.

If there is no one special in your life at this time, you should still prepare the shell for when that someone does enter your life. When you do give it to someone, the person will be instantly smitten with you.

Seashells haunt with love

INCANTATION

> *Dead men of the sea,*
> *Listen as I speak.*
> *Whisper into this shell,*
> *My name to repeat.*
> *Haunt it with my presence,*
> *Power it with the sea.*
> *I shall thank you always,*
> *For bringing love to me.*
> *So Mote It Be.*

To Make a Man Confess His Love for You

Love Dreams

TIME   Waxing Friday, Venus hour.

TOOLS   One pink candle, Venus oil, Lover's incense, a pillowcase, water, cinnamon, bloodroot, witch's grass, and a red mojo.

INSTRUCTIONS   Anoint the candle with Venus oil; light the candle and incense.

Wash the pillowcase carefully in a mixture of water, cinnamon, and bloodroot. Suffumigate the pillowcase with the incense smoke. Place the witch's grass in the red mojo.

Anoint the pillowcase with Venus oil and then kiss it. Recite the incantation.

Keep the pillowcase in your lingerie drawer next to the mojo for three days.

On the night of the full moon, give the pillowcase to your lover as a gift. Do not have sex with him until he confesses how much he loves you. He will tell you before three moons have passed. You can seal the spell with a sexual encounter after he tells you he loves you—but this is only a suggestion.

INCANTATION

A cloth of magick has been weaved,
A spell of love has been conceived.
Washed in cinnamon and then in blood,
Dried in the smoke of infinite love.
Patiently wait for three nights to pass,
Absorb the passion of witch's grass.
Anoint with Venus and bestow a kiss,
And give my lover this special gift.
When the globe is round and high,
The beacon of love will light the sky.
His heart now full with love to confess,
For he cannot sleep and he cannot rest.
Visions of me will haunt his head,
In his dreams and in his bed.
His love cannot wait for it must be told,
Before three moons have turned cold.
When at last the words have been said,
I'll warm his heart and then his bed.
The cloth of magick has served me well,
Granted by Goddess in my love dream spell.
So Mote It Be.

To Make an Old Lover Return to You

13, 12, 10, and 9

TIME   Hare Moon, Venus hour.

TOOLS   A horseshoe, dragon's blood reed, khus-khus, a buckeye, a picture of your old lover, a pink votive candle with your ex's name carved into the bottom, an orange votive candle, Bewitching oil, a combination of Come to Me and Irresistible incense. Obtain additional pink and orange votives for later.

INSTRUCTIONS   During the Venus hour of the Hare Moon, take thirteen steps outside your home in a northern direction. Dig a hole approximately ten inches deep. Bury inside the horseshoe, the dragon's blood reed, khus-khus, the buckeye, and the picture of your ex in the hole. Fill it in and draw a nine-inch circle around it. Set the pink and orange votives on top of the hole and anoint them with Bewitching oil and place the combination of incenses on top of the hole. At midnight, go back outside and light the candles and the incense. Recite the incantation. Leave the lit candles to go out naturally. For the remaining fourteen nights, light pink and orange candles to draw him nearer to you. He shall be there before the next full moon.

INCANTATION

> *Forest of trees, hear my cry,*
> *Send this message through the midnight sky.*
> *Return to me [his name,] I need him near,*
> *Pierce his mind and bring him here.*
> *The hare moon now marks the time,*
> *Of 13, 12, 10, and 9.*
> *The spell is cast and the Earth awaits,*
> *Bring [his name] back, it is his fate.*
> *Angels of Love, hear my plea,*
> *Bring my true love back to me.*
> *Love can't wait, for I am bound,*
> *Bring him here before the moon doeth round.*
> *So Mote It Be.*

To Bring About a Romantic Relationship
Guys and Dolls

TIME   Waxing Friday, Venus hour.

TOOLS   A pink image candle in the form of the sex of the person you'd like to attract, Lover's oil, Come to Me incense, cinnamon, rose petals, one peach pit, High John the Conqueror root, aloes, lady's mantle, one pink quartz, and a red mojo.

INSTRUCTIONS   Anoint the image candle with Lover's oil. Light the candle and the incense. Place all of the herbs, rose petals, the peach pit, and the quartz in the red mojo. Suffumigate the mojo deosil in the incense while reciting the incantation. Place the mojo under your pillow each night until your new friend enters your life. When

A male image candle

he or she does enter, throw your mojo in a large body of water. Thank the Goddess for the person that She brought to you. Until then, light the image candle every day at a Venus hour for approximately ten minutes each time when the moon is waxing. Recite the incantation each time you burn the candle. When the moon is waning, keep your image candle beneath your bed and do nothing with it. Make sure that you visualize love knocking at your door when you light your image candle. This is a lengthy spell, but a good one. If love does not not enter your life within the burning of one image candle, you can anoint another image candle and try again. You can do this for up to three candles. This is an excellent time to join a singles' club or place an ad in the personals. You will attract all sorts of people, so make sure that you're focusing on the right kind of relationship.

INCANTATION

Guys and Dolls, come out to play,
You cannot resist what I say.
Come to Me and Lover's ascend,
Venus waxing as love transcends.
Goddess has chosen my perfect romance,
Search and seek where my love enchants.
Pretty pink statues of Dolls and Guys,
Burn the flame with no disguise.
The pathway lit to bring you here,
You are drawn to me without fear.
Within this magickal purse of scarlet,
Resides the potion of the harlot.
Seek, search, clamor, and climb,
To my heart and there you'll find,
Eternal love, passions, and joy,
Find me now, my little love toy.
Your only thoughts are to be with me,
This is my will, So Mote It Be.

To Become More Beautiful on the Outside

Beauty Bath in the Grass

TIME   Full Moon, Venus hour.

TOOLS   One pink candle, Goddess oil, Lovely incense, and a beautiful, lush, green lawn.

INSTRUCTIONS   Anoint the candle with Goddess oil; light the candle and the incense. Walk to the lush green lawn in the light of the full moon completely naked before the Goddess. Carry the candle and the incense. Wash your hair, your face, your body—everything down to your toes—in the dew on the grass. Keep your eyes on the moon. If clouds cover it, put your robe on and run for shelter (it's a bad omen to bathe beneath a cloud-covered moon). When you've finished your bath, recite the incantation under the moon. Beauty will radiate from you.

INCANTATION

> *Venus high and Venus low,*
> *Bring me beauty in your flow.*
> *Goddess bestow an earthly kiss,*
> *So I can feel Your gentle lips.*
> *Grant me beauty with*
>   *the Moon of Milk,*
> *Luster my hair with glorious silk.*
> *Skin and eyes, clear will shine,*
> *Twin my image to look like Thine.*
> *Goddess of beauty, wisdom,*
>   *and grace,*
> *Place Thy beauty upon my face.*
> *So Mote It Be.*

To Promote Romantic Love

Love Strings

TIME   Full Moon, Venus hour.

TOOLS   One pink candle, Dove's Blood oil, Sweetheart incense, thirteen pink beads, and a black cord that measures about two feet.

INSTRUCTIONS   Carve your lover's initials in the pink candle and anoint the candle with Dove's Blood oil. Light the candle and the incense. Concentrate on your lover becoming more attentive and romantic.

While reciting the incantation, tie a knot on one end of the black cord, then slide a pink bead on and tie another knot. Do this for the remaining twelve beads (the pattern should be knot, bead, knot, bead, and so on). Pass the string through the incense smoke.

Wear the string as a side belt (if you are wearing a regular belt, drape the string over the belt on your side so it folds in half). He will not resist you while you are wearing your love strings.

INCANTATION

> Knot bead one, the spell has begun.
> Knot bead two, he will feel it, too.
> Knot bead three, he loves only me.
> Knot bead four, it is me he adores.
> Knot bead five, this spell is alive.
> Knot bead six, his attentions are fixed.
> Knot bead seven, take me to heaven.
> Knot bead eight, it is his fate.
> Knot bead nine, his love is now mine.
> Knot bead ten, there is no end.
> Knot bead eleven, Goddess in heaven.
> Knot bead twelve, he's under my spell.

Knot bead thirteen, his love is working.
Belted to my side in two,
His love is secure in all we do.
So Mote It Be.

To Stabilize Good Friendships

Four Season Friends

TIME   Hare Moon, Venus hour.

TOOLS   Three pink candles, Sweetpea oil, Merry Meet incense, mortar and pestle, jasmine, sunflower, sweetpea, honey, cinnamon, a lemon, and four cups of talcum powder.

INSTRUCTIONS   Anoint the three pink candles with Sweetpea oil. Light the candles and the incense. With a mortar and pestle, grind the jasmine, sunflower, and sweetpea together. Add in honey, cinnamon, and the juice of a fresh lemon. Mix together. Spread the mixture into a thin layer and allow it to dry.

After thirty minutes has passed, recite the incantation. In an earthen bowl, combine four cups of talcum powder with the mixture and recite the incantation again. Let this dry for three days.

Wear it as a friendship powder all over your body. It will stabilize good friendships and attract new ones.

INCANTATION

Hidden moon that grows to wax,
Friendships golden soon attract.
Frolic to the tune of Merry,
Laughter and joy will always carry.
Honest friendships are the reasons,
I seek the truth in all four seasons.
Mask of betrayal will stay at bay,

Only good friends will come my way.
So Mote It Be.

To Attract and Arouse Male Interest

Friday Night Sender

TIME   Waxing Friday, Venus hour.

TOOLS   A pink candle, Aphrodisia oil, Jezebel incense, a garnet, ginseng, ginger, a red mojo, and red silk.

Mojo and garnet

INSTRUCTIONS Anoint the candle with Aphrosidia oil. Light the candle and the incense. Sew or glue a garnet onto your clothing. Anoint the pulse points of your body and wear the Aphrodisia oil along with your perfume. Put the herbs into the mojo, seal it, and roll it up tight. Fold the mojo inside of the red silk and tie it around your left ankle. (If you are wearing pants, chances are this will not be seen. If you are wearing a dress, make the decoration around your ankle pretty.) Recite the incantation. Go out and rest assured that all kinds of male attention will be cast upon you. Feel confident and enjoy the attention.

INCANTATION

> *Waxing Venus, waxing beauty, waxing pink,*
> *The heads will turn, the eyes will wink.*
> *Unleash the powers of love and lust,*
> *Consume my body with confidence and trust.*
> *To all of those that are male in gender,*
> *Come to me, the Friday Night Sender.*
> *You have no choice, I hold your key,*
> *The only female to have is me.*
> *The potion attracts all males of desire,*
> *Drink in the love to quench the fire.*
> *So Mote It Be.*

TO PROMOTE WEIGHT LOSS

Shrinking Violets

TIME Full Moon, Sun hour.

TOOLS One large pink candle, Venus oil, Lovely incense, and one very healthy African violet.

INSTRUCTIONS This is a continuous spell that you do until you have reached the weight you want. Anoint the candle with the

Venus oil. Light the candle and the incense. Set the African Violet near the pink candle. Focus your sight on the violet and see it as yourself: beautiful, delicate, and properly proportioned. Starting at your navel area, take your power hand and, with your palm facing you, make ever-widening deosil circles while reciting the first incantation. Then reverse the rotation in a widdershins motion and make the circles smaller and smaller, ending at the navel area while reciting the second incantation. Do this every day at the Sun hour until you have achieved the look you desire. Visualize your tummy becoming smaller and tighter. Focus your eyes on the beautiful African violet. As the pink candle becomes smaller and smaller, so will you.

INCANTATION 1

> *Healthy and well my body will be,*
> *Strong and stable in harmony.*
> *So Mote It Be.*

INCANTATION 2

> *Waning in size and hunger free,*
> *Smaller and smaller, tighter be.*
> *So Mote It Be.*

TO ASK THE GODDESS FOR BLESSINGS

The Female Self-Blessing

TIME   Full Moon, Jupiter hour.

TOOLS   One pink candle, Goddess oil, Goddess incense, rosewater, a clear quartz crystal, and a rose quartz.

INSTRUCTIONS   This spell is to be performed skyclad.
Anoint the candle with Goddess oil. Light the candle and the incense. Center yourself and align your chakras.

Recite the incantation while holding the clear quartz in your left hand and the rose quartz in your right. Anoint both of these stones with rosewater when it is called for in the incantation. When the spell is complete, place both of the crystals in a garden. You shall soon have the feeling that the Goddess is shining special favor upon you and a warm feeling of self-love.

INCANTATION

> *Lady of Light, so fair and so kind,*
> *I humbly bow before you.*
> *[Anoint the rose quartz with rosewater]*
> *Lady of Love, so gentle and serene,*
> *I ask for blessings from you.*
> *[Anoint the clear quartz with rosewater]*
> *Lady of Power, Mother of Earth,*
> *I pledge my eternal devotion.*
> *[Anoint the rose quartz with rosewater]*
> *Lady of Healing, so giving and free,*
> *I ask to love and to cherish myself.*
> *[Anoint the clear quartz with rosewater]*
> *Lady of Sight, our loving Mother,*
> *I surrender all that I have.*
> *[Anoint the rose quartz with rosewater]*
> *Lady of Women, Goddess of All,*
> *I ask to be worthy of your love.*
> *[Anoint the clear quartz with rosewater]*
> *Together these stones represent me,*
> *I ask for self-love and your blessings.*
> *May I grow and flourish in your eyes,*
> *May I always be within your heart.*
> *[Anoint both stones with Goddess oil]*
> *This is my will, So Mote It Be.*

5

SPELLS THAT ARE *Red*

> Passions of scarlet bundled in red,
> Entrancing those who dare to tread.
> Upon the coals that burn and blaze,
> Forever frenzied with lusting craze.
> —Belladonna

The color red represents magick involving unencumbered energy, physical and mental strength, passion, lust, fast action, anger, impulsiveness, and erratic behavior.

To Arouse a Man's Passion

Mountain Madness

TIME   Waxing Friday, Venus hour.

TOOLS   Love seed, lavender, Jezebel root, parsley, passionflower, a red candle, Sheba oil, Eve incense, mortar and pestle, a red flannel mojo, and a bottle of red wine.

INSTRUCTIONS   With mortar and pestle, grind all the herbs together so that they are powdered. Anoint the red candle with Sheba oil and light both the candle and incense. Place the powdered herbs in the red mojo, but do not permanently seal it, and recite the incantation over the herbs.

Take your man to a secluded area in nature for a picnic. In your picnic basket, have whatever you want to eat, along with your bottle of red wine and the red mojo. Also include a soft blanket to picnic on. After the wine has been opened, secretly place a pinch of the herbs into his cup and softly recite the incantation again. Have him drink the brew and be ready for the passion to begin.

INCANTATION

> Lusting herbs of southern sky,
> Release your magick where they lie.
> Love and passion now unfold,
> Tales and secrets never told.
> Western sky in all delight,
> Bring the love I have in sight.
> Strong and tender he shall be,
> When a sip of wine enters thee.
> So Mote It Be.

For Releasing Anger, Pain, Grief, or Jealousy

Scarlet Letter

TIME   Waning Tuesday, Mars hour.

TOOLS   One red candle, Uncrossing oil, Dragon's Blood incense, a red pen, white parchment, chili powder, black pepper, an envelope, and a cauldron.

INSTRUCTIONS   Anoint the candle with Uncrossing oil. Light the candle and the incense.

With pen and parchment, write a letter to the God expressing why you want to rid yourself of any negative emotions. Explain why you no longer need these emotions and how you wish to be free from them. End the letter with *So Mote It Be* and sign your name. Place chili powder and black pepper inside the letter and seal it in the envelope. Pass the letter widdershins through the incense smoke and recite the incantation. Ignite the letter in the candle's flame and toss it into the cauldron.

After it burns up, the ashes must be taken to water that flows away from your home and be tossed in.

The red letter

INCANTATION

Red as Mars,
Scarlet letter.
Remove the scars,
For the better.
Banish the pain,
Return to burn.
Happy to gain,
Grace to learn.
So Mote It Be.

To Arouse Your Own Passion

Surrender

TIME   Create this brew on a Hare Moon, Moon hour. You may save this brew and use it anytime during the waxing moon.

TOOLS   A red candle, Fire of Passion oil and incense, petals from a red rose, bloodroot, gentian, damiana, jasmine, and a red mojo.

INSTRUCTIONS   Anoint the candle with the Fire of Passion oil. Light the candle and the incense. Blend all the herbs together and grind them into a powder. Recite the incantation. Place the herbs in the red mojo.

When ready to have a night of passion, light the incense and the candle. Draw a warm bath and place all the herbs into the bathwater. Recite the incantation again. Let loose and have some fun.

INCANTATION

Sleeping passion slumber no more,
Release the lust in which I store.
Light the tickle within my loins,
Spark the fire that passion joins.
Brew of water, brew of flame,

Release the lust of wicked dames.
Caress the heart and body so tender,
Let my soul completely surrender.
So Mote It Be.

For Courage

The Pyramid

TIME   Hare Moon, Mars hour.

TOOLS   One red candle, Q incense, Mandrake oil, a pen with red ink, white parchment, a pyramid, and a magnifying glass.

Pyramid power

INSTRUCTIONS   Anoint the candle with Mandrake oil. Light the candle and the incense. With the red pen, write on the parchment what you need to have courage for and what you would like to see result from your courage. For example, "I would like to have the courage to ask my employer for a raise. I would like to have a significant increase in my salary effective today." Place the parchment under the pyramid. Suspend the magnifying glass above the pyramid. Visualize an enormous rush of courage coming over you. Feel the heat. Visualize the result you desire. Recite the incantation. Leave the spell intact until you receive the courage. After you have acted, light the paper using the red candle and disperse the ashes into the wind.

(Remember to keep the magnifying glass away from sunlight so it does not catch anything on fire.)

INCANTATION

> Pyramid of almighty power,
> Expand courage from your tower.
> Grant me with the scarlet nerve,
> Success in all that I deserve.
> Grand and growing is the flame,
> To move forward without shame.
> Omnipotent in all I skill,
> Courage abounds my free will.
> So Mote It Be.

To Arouse His Passion

Oil to Boil

TIME   Full Moon, Venus hour.

TOOLS   A red candle, a dash of Arabian Nights oil, Rendezvous incense, a mandrake root, a dash of Passion oil, a dash of French love oil, 3/4 cup of almond oil, cinnamon oil, and a pink or red bottle in which to store the oil.

INSTRUCTIONS Anoint the red candle with Arabian Nights oil. Light the candle and the incense. Place the mandrake root and all the oils in the colored bottle and stir deosil. Recite the incantation. When the moment is right, give your man a massage by candlelight (use a red candle), using the brew that you created as your massage oil.

Potion for massage

INCANTATION

In my hands this magick brew,
Touch with fire when I ask of you.
Warmer, warmer, until it flames,
When I touch what once was lame.
Oil to boil with passion and lust,
To touch my body is a must.
Rise up to be rigid and strong,
Endure the passion all night long.
So Mote It Be.

For Endurance During Difficult Times

Rising Steam

TIME   Waxing Tuesday, Sun hour (this spell works best when cast in advance of a difficult situation).

TOOLS   One red candle, Wolf Song oil, Dragon's Blood incense, four cups of water, an earthen pot, three pinches of salt, and an airtight jar with lid.

INSTRUCTIONS   Anoint the candle with Wolf Song oil. Light the candle and the incense. Visualize yourself smiling with confidence.

Place four cups of water in an earthen pot and bring it to a boil. Cast in three pinches of salt. Add three drops of Wolf Song oil. Recite the incantation.

As the water begins to boil, catch the steam in the jar and seal it tight. Whenever you feel the need, open the jar and rub the condensation from the steam across your forehead. No matter what the situation, you will be able to mentally and emotionally endure it.

INCANTATION

Dragons with red fiery eyes,
Breathe the flame to neutralize.

Diminish the pain with the sweat,
Across my forehead with no regret.
Endurance is what I invite,
Till my senses reunite.
I call upon the rising steam,
Perseverance intervene.
So Mote It Be.

Potion for endurance

To Increase Physical Strength

Lightning

TIME   During any electrical storm.

TOOLS   One red candle, Double Action oil, Violet incense, a bay leaf, masterwort, pennyroyal, earthen bowl, plastic wrap, a carpenter's nail, and a red mojo.

INSTRUCTIONS   Anoint the candle with Double Action oil. Light the candle and the incense. Grind together bay leaf, masterwort, and pennyroyal. Place them in an earthen bowl and cover it with plastic wrap. Place the carpenter's nail point-down in the very center of the bowl, piercing the plastic wrap. The nail should be upright. Recite the incantation. Place the bowl outside to absorb the power of the storm.

When the storm has subsided, place the nail and herbs in the red mojo. Place the mojo beneath the shoes you wear when you are exercising or in need of physical strength.

INCANTATION

> Earth. Earth. Earth.
> Air. Air. Air.
> Fire. Fire. Fire.
> Water. Water. Water.
> Earth, Air, Fire, Water.
> Earth, Air, Fire, Water.
> Earth, Air, Fire, Water.
> With the power of three times three,
> Strength. Strength. Strength.
> Lightning. Lightning. Lightning.
> So Mote It Be.

To Light Your Own Fire and Stir Your Female Passion

The Female Meltdown

TIME   Full Moon, Venus hour.

TOOLS   One red female image candle, Cleopatra oil, Passion incense, a cauldron, ten ounces of red wine or cherry cider, two pinches of finely powdered domania, and two pinches of finely powdered cubeb berries.

INSTRUCTIONS   Anoint the female image candle with Cleopatra oil. (Beware: Cleo is a hot mama, and this oil is extremely flammable.) Place two ounces of your wine or cider in a large cast-iron cauldron. (Place a potholder beneath the cauldron if you're casting this inside.) Place the image candle in the cauldron also. Light the candle and the incense. Sprinkle half of the herbs in the remaining wine or cider. Recite the incantation over it. Sprinkle the remaining half of the herbs on the burning image candle. Recite the incantation again. As you watch the image candle burn, visualize all of your problems melting away. Drink the brew. As you are visualizing yourself in the most positive way, see your chakras glowing. Each and every chakra is getting red and hot, exploding within your body. Feel the heat rise from your loins and up toward your head. As this image grows stronger, surrender to the passionate goddess within you. Unleash yourself as the candle melts to liquid. After the wax has cooled (and you have too), roll it into a ball and use it again when you are in need of a boost of passion. Simply heat the ball of wax and melt it down again.

INCANTATION

> *Scarlet image bares no shame,*
> *Sensuality is what I claim.*

Slowly melting away with time,
There is no rush for potion wine.
Generously adorned with passion herbs,
Caressing my body with velvet words.
Inspired by Cleopatra's ways,
Lusting thoughts embrace my days.
Open the door within myself,
Reach the valley of erotic wealth.
Seducing candle with dancing flame,
Release your magick within this dame.
So Mote It Be.

For the female Witch to be-Witch herself

6

SPELLS THAT ARE
Orange

> Hypnotic music seduces the ear,
> They hum the tune as they draw near.
> They cannot explain nor escape,
> What draws them to the Witch's cape.
> —Belladonna

The color orange represents magick involving attraction, compelling others to do your bidding, enticement, real estate, and bending laws.

TO SOLICIT A GRAY WITCH OF YESTERYEAR TO AID YOU IN ANY POSITIVE MAGICKAL ENDEAVOR

The Witch of the Well

TIME   Full Moon, Moon hour.

TOOLS   A white candle, Honeysuckle oil, and Mojo incense

INSTRUCTIONS   Anoint the white candle with the Honeysuckle oil and light it. Using the light of the Full Moon and your candlelight, find an old well that still has water in it (please be careful not to fall in). Legend says that the souls of Gray Witches are inside the wells. They have passed out of their time dimension, but need to serve one wish for a White Witch before they can be released into Heaven. The granting of the wish will complete their karmic commitment to the Craft.

Light the Mojo incense. Peer down into the well and summon the Gray Witch with the incantation. After the Gray Witch has assisted you with your spell, you must declare the task before the Goddess and God with the second incantation. It is important to recite this incantation as soon as the Gray Witch has completed your wish. If you wait or delay, you will soon have your spell reversed.

INCANTATION 1

> *I call to you, Gray Witch of the Well!*
> *I need for you to assist my spell.*
> *I know this task will set you free,*
> *To the Heavens of eternity.*
> *This is my wish, this is your task,*
> *I need [state your wish], is what I ask.*
> *So Mote It Be!*

INCANTATION 2

> *The Witch of Gray that was in this well,*
> *Has successfully aided my one-wish spell.*
> *Find her place, give her a crown,*
> *For aiding me in drawing the moon down!*
> *No longer novice of serving in gray,*
> *A White Witch comes before you this day.*
> *So Mote It Be.*

To Attract a New Love to Your Life

Pinning Him

Time   Full Moon, Venus hour.

Tools   One pink taper candle, Sweetpea oil, Scorpion incense, thirteen straight pins, some with pink heads and some with orange heads, and a wind chime with a soft tone.

Instructions   Anoint the pink taper candle with the Sweetpea oil. Light the candle and the incense. Stick the thirteen pins in the candle. Recite the incantation while passing the candle and the wind chime through the incense. Place the wind chime in a window in your home that has southern exposure. Let your candle burn down all the way and throw the remaining wax into flowing water. Every time you hear the soft tinkle of your wind chime, you will know that your love is getting closer and closer to you.

Incantation

> *I pin my new love with a*
>   *pledge and a song,*
> *Hear the music and sing along.*
> *My love is open and I compel your heart,*
> *I pin my love so [he or she] will never part.*
> *I call upon my lover and my mate,*
> *Come to me now, no longer wait.*
> *Listen to the South winds play,*
> *A lover's sonnet compels you today.*
> *I pin my new love, my heart's desire,*
> *Enter my arms and romance the fire.*
> *So Mote It Be.*

To Attract Customers to a Business

Call the Customers

Time   Waxing Thursday, Jupiter hour.

Tools   One large orange candle, one large green candle, Scorpion oil, Drawing incense, a blue flag root, basil, three pecans, and a red mojo.

Instructions   Anoint both candles with Scorpion oil. Light the candles and the incense. Place the blue flag root, the basil, and the three pecans in the red mojo. Pass the mojo through the smoke of the Drawing incense and recite the incantation.

Place the mojo in the cash register drawer. Customers will flock to your business before the moon is full.

Incantation

> *I call upon the Jupiter hour,*
> *To aid me during this time of power.*
> *Three herbs are calling from the cradle,*
> *To bring the business of which I'm able.*
> *Blessed by flame of orange and green,*
> *Enchant the people of which I need.*
> *Compel their flow, compel their friends,*
> *Send me business that will never end.*
> *I trust the Scorpion to place the call,*
> *Attract me customers most of all.*
> *Draw them in and draw them well,*
> *This business I ask to compel.*
> *So Mote It Be.*

To Receive a Response

Ring Me

TIME   Hare Moon, Mercury hour.

TOOLS   One large orange candle, Cornucopia oil, Come to Me incense, white parchment, a writing pen with orange ink, and a sewing needle.

INSTRUCTIONS   Anoint the candle with Cornucopia oil. Light the candle and the incense. On the white parchment, write in orange ink the name of the person you desire to call you. (The reason behind the call is not as important as getting the call to happen now.) Draw a circle around the name of the person and pierce it with the sewing needle. Take this over to your phone and say the person's name out loud. Place the parchment on top of the phone. Recite the incantation.

INCANTATION

> *[Person's name], I call upon you!*
> *Return with message*
>   *upon this cue.*
> *Your face I see, your voice I hear,*
> *Call me now with words so clear.*
> *Make it happen, see my face,*
> *Hasten the call, hasten your pace.*
> *Ring my phone, ring my bell,*
> *You cannot resist this*
>   *magickal spell.*
> *So Mote It Be.*

To Gain Major Influence Over People

High John, Low John

TIME   Full Moon, Moon hour.

TOOLS   One orange candle, Bewitching oil, French Quarter Creole incense, sixteen ounces of talc, earthen bowl, one High John root, one Low John root, a pinch of devil's shoestring, and one red mojo.

INSTRUCTIONS   Anoint the candle with Bewitching oil. Light the candle and the incense. Place the talc in an earthen bowl. Grind the High John, Low John, and devil's shoestring into a powder and mix well. Recite the incantation. Place the powder in the mojo until you are ready to use it.

The powder is to be placed on your hands if shaking hands with the person you want to influence, or sprinkled into the shoes of someone you want to influence, all of which is to be done without the other person's knowledge.

INCANTATION

> *Place the strings from devil's shoes,*
> *In the ashes of John's brew.*
> *Stir them deosil, grind them well,*
> *Touch hand or sole to compel.*
> *Power of John, high and low,*
> *Conquer, conquest, head to toe.*
> *Think me great, think me swell,*
> *Now I have you under my spell.*
> *So Mote It Be.*

To Attract Good Luck

Cabbage Patch Baby

TIME   Waxing Thursday, Jupiter hour.

TOOLS   One orange candle, Follow Me oil, Fast Luck incense, dried cabbage, two cotton balls, Irish moss, poppyseeds, clover, one baby sock, and orange thread.

INSTRUCTIONS   Anoint the candle with Follow Me oil. Light the candle and the incense. Place the cabbage, cotton balls, irish moss, poppy seeds, and clover inside the baby sock. Sew the sock closed with the orange thread. Recite the incantation. Pass the sock deosil through the incense smoke.

Place the sock over the threshold of your home in an inconspicuous place. Good luck will be attracted to you. You can reenergize your spell by placing it in the light of the full moon every month.

INCANTATION

> *Luck of Irish,*
> *Poppycock.*
> *Twins of cotton,*
> *Leafy shamrock.*
> *Cabbage foliage,*
> *Baby's sock.*
> *Over the doorsill,*
> *Good luck knocks.*
> *So Mote It Be.*

To Attract a Spouse

Merry Maiden, Marry Maiden

TIME   Full Moon, Venus hour.

TOOLS   Maidenhair, fresh mountain water, a map of the state in which you wish to live, a pink candle, Marriage Mind oil, Dove's Blood incense, a wedding band, and an orange ribbon.

INSTRUCTIONS   Wash your hair with shampoo and rinse with maidenhair and fresh mountain water. Go into a wooded area near your home. Nail the map of the state in which you would like to live to a tree. Anoint your candle with Marriage Mind oil. Light the candle and the incense. Call upon the Goddess to bring your new mate to you. Anoint yourself with the oil too. Dance around the tree and recite the incantation. Place the gold band on the orange ribbon and hang it from the tree. The Goddess will show you where your mate is.

You must search the city and rural areas that the Goddess impressed upon you to find this perfect mate. You must wear the oil as a perfume when searching for him. If you search as the Goddess instructs you, your mate will be found within three full moons.

INCANTATION

> *Merry Maiden, Merry Me,*
> *I offer my love to this tree.*
> *I dance, I prance, with love's delight,*
> *Bring my mate upon this night.*
> *Merry Maiden, Marry Me.*
> *I ask for love from this tree.*
> *Goddess of light, Goddess above,*
> *Please send me to the one I love.*
> *My mate, my man, bring him to me,*
> *From maiden, to promise, to bride-to-be.*

I pledge myself to my spouse so true,
I dance, I prance, I sing to you.
Love divine with this band of gold,
Lead me to the mate I'll hold.
This merry maiden holds the band,
That leads me to my promised man.
Guide me Goddess, lead the way,
Take me to my wedding day.
Merry Maiden, Marry Me,
Take me to my husband to be.
So Mote It Be.

7

SPELLS THAT ARE *Green*

> Valleys and meadows in silent stealth,
> Swelling abundance of the wealth.
> Fertile faeries with waxing sheen,
> Plush and bountiful blankets of green.
> —Belladonna

The color green represents magick involving money of any kind, prosperity, business increase, good luck, fertility, growth, attainment of financial goals, employment, and expansion.

TO BLESS A BUSINESS WITH SUCCESS

Seven, Seven, and Seven

TIME   Waxing Sunday, Jupiter hour.

TOOLS   One green seven-knob candle (see illustration), Prosperity oil, Better Business incense, a flowerpot, and a forget-me-not plant.

INSTRUCTIONS   Anoint the candle with Prosperity oil. Light the candle and the incense. Visualize customers coming to the business and cash overflowing the cash register. Recite the incantation seven times during a seven-hour burning. You can encourage the candle to burn quickly so the remains of the candle are less than one knob. (If for any reason the candle does not burn all the way within the seven hours, then try the spell again.) Place the remains of the candle in the base of the pot and plant the forget-me-not on top of it. Keep the plant at the place of business at all times.

INCANTATION

> *To ensure the business with success,*
> *A seven-knob candle now to dress.*
> *With Prosperity oil from foot to nape,*
> *Better Business encircles the fate.*
> *Day of the Sun and Jupiter hour,*
> *Bestow the magick and the power.*
> *For seven hours it must burn,*
> *And seven words now be learned.*
> *Success, abundance, prosperity,*
> *Faith, hope, and charity.*
> *Seven hours is the test,*
> *All the candle burned is best.*
> *If any whole knob yet remain,*
> *Invest the spell and do again.*
> *Practice the heart for purity,*
> *Share with love and certainty.*
> *Seven knobs must all compress,*
> *To have assurance of the success.*
> *Place the remains within the pot,*
> *That sprouts a lively forget-me-not.*
> *Within the business it shall flourish,*
> *Attracting customers, it will nourish.*

Thrive with faith, hope, and charity,
For success, abundance, and prosperity.
So Mote It Be.

Seven-knob wishing candle

To Get a Specific Job

The Offering

Time   The first part needs to be done on a Waxing Sunday, Jupiter hour. The second part needs to be done on a Waxing Thursday, Jupiter hour.

Tools   One green candle, Woodland oil, Helping Hand incense, basil, rattlesnake root, vervain, an earthen bowl, and seven pennies.

Instructions   Anoint the candle with Woodland oil. Light the candle and the incense. On the waxing Sunday, at Jupiter hour, combine the basil, rattlesnake root, and vervain in an earthen bowl. Pray to St. Joseph over the herbs to receive the employment you desire. Leave the bowl undisturbed until the waxing Thursday.

On that Thursday, at Jupiter hour, go to the place you would like to work. Bring the bowl of herbs, the candle, and the incense. Place the herbs on the ground in a small pile. Light the candle and the incense. Anoint the herbs with the Woodland oil. Pray to the Goddess and God that this employment be yours. Place seven pennies around the herbs in a circle and recite the incantation. Take only the candle and incense burner back home with you; leave the herbs, burned incense, and pennies on the ground. The job should be yours within one lunar cycle.

This spell can also be done by proxy at your home if you can't do it at the actual job site. You will need to draw a map that includes a picture of the building complete with the address and some soil to place on top of the picture of the building. The spell can then be completed. Take the little job site and put it safely away after the spell is cast.

Incantation

> *Cut a slice of St. John's bread,*
> *On the day of the sun, we shall all be fed.*
> *Add the buttons of the rattlesnake,*

Pink candles in the trees make strong magick for calling in love from far away.

Waterfall magick is very powerful when releasing bad habits or unwanted relationships.

The athame can vary in size from three inches long to three feet long.

Castings for blue when asking for protection or peace.

When brewing healing potions, don't forget your water and lemons for cleansing.

Two pink roses with a seashell will haunt lovers with romantic thoughts.

Serious sex magick invokes all the red energies.

A green altar is prepared when casting for money.

Amethyst adorns the purple altar when conjuring for psychic abilities.

The Goddess is adorned by gold when conjuring for success.

When brewing for court magick, many Egyptian spells are used.

The smoldering chalice entices Witches to conjure soon.

Preparing for the Esbat.

The cauldron is always in the center of the coven's circle.

Combine with Van Van and pray to the Saint.
On the day of Jupiter in the waxing light,
Consecrate the work place in the shadows of night.
Place the potion upon the ground,
Light the candle to draw the moon down.
Anoint the threshold in the Woodlands,
Burn the smoke of the Helping Hands.
Pray to Goddess and God that be,
For work and gain and prosperity.
Upon your leave offer the coins of seven,
To protect the potion while under heaven.
The abundance of Jupiter will do the rest,
So Mote It Be and So Be Blessed.

Pennies under heaven

To Become Pregnant

Blessed Enchantment

TIME   Full Moon, Sun hour.

TOOLS   A green candle, a pink candle, Fertility oil, Huntress incense, figs, dates, nuts, cucumbers, olives, a geranium, and access to a pine tree.

INSTRUCTIONS   Anoint the candles with Fertility oil. Light both candles and the incense. Serve a plate of figs, dates, nuts, cucumbers, and olives. Eat them with your spouse while reciting the incantation. Place the geranium under the bed in which the child is to be conceived.

Dig a hole near a pine tree and place a piece of the geranium and the ashes from the incense in the hole. Recite the incantation while filling in the hole.

INCANTATION

> *The enchantment begins*
>   *under the full moon,*
> *When a child will be conceived real soon.*
> *Figs, nuts, cucumbers, olives, and dates,*
> *Will inspire fertility while we mate.*
> *Geranium placed beneath the bed,*
> *Will secure good fortune lies ahead.*
> *Dusted smoke and geranium flower,*
> *Beneath the pine will give power.*
> *The blessed enchantment will soon*
>   *have birth,*
> *With thanks and praise to Goddess and earth.*
> *So Mote It Be.*

To Sell a House

Little Green Apples

TIME To be completed during the waxing phase of the Moon.

TOOLS A rock and some grass from the property you want to sell, a St. Christopher's medallion, ten inches of green string and enough orange beads to fill the string, star anise, and a whole nutmeg.

INSTRUCTIONS Obtain a rock from your property you want to sell. Take some grass from the same property and stain the rock with it while visualizing selling your home. See the contract and the handshake of the sale. Take the rock to rapidly-moving water that flows away from the property. Throw the rock in the water and again visualize the sale.

Take the St. Christopher's medallion and bury it head-first in your front yard. Pray that the house will sell quickly.

Put the orange beads on the green string and tie it into a circle. Place the string around the knob on the inside of the front door. Visualize money touching the door handle. Keep this on the door until the house sells.

Place star anise in all four corners of the inside of the house—be sure it is a significant amount. Carry a whole nutmeg with you at all times (all the owners must do this, if there is more than one owner). It must be with you wherever you go (in a purse, pocket, wallet, etc.). Visualize the signing of the contract every time you touch or think about the nutmeg.

After the property is sold, dig up the St. Christopher medallion, and in its place bury the beads, the star anise, and the nutmeg. Give thanks for the contract while you are burying these items. This spell works extremely fast and effectively if followed through correctly.

So Mote It Be.

To Win at Gambling

Gambler's Gloves

TIME   Create this spell on a waxing Sunday, Jupiter hour.

TOOLS   Three green candles, Fast Luck oil, Lady Luck incense, five finger grass, spearmint, nutmeg, verbena, star anise, seven green job's tears, one cup of talc, and a red mojo.

INSTRUCTIONS   Anoint the three green candles with Fast Luck oil. Light the candles and the incense. Combine all of the herbs in a bowl. Say the incantation over the herbs. Add one dram of Fast Luck oil to the herbs; then add the cup of talc and place the entire ingredients in the red mojo. Pass the mojo through the incense smoke.

When you are ready to gamble, light the candles and incense, and pass the mojo deosil through the smoke. Rub some of the contents of the mojo into your hands. Recite the incantation again, and do not wash your hands, or you will wash off the good luck. Secretly carry the mojo with you while gambling.

INCANTATION

> *Waxing Jupiter and waxing Sun,*
> *Bless my hands so they have won.*
> *Fast Luck and the Lady will cheer,*
> *Gain and fortune with Job's tears.*
> *I wash my hands with luck and love,*
> *Win me big with the gambling gloves.*
> *So Mote It Be.*

To Bring Prosperity

A Pirate's Passage

TIME   Begin on Hare Moon, Jupiter hour.

TOOLS   One green candle, Mermaid's Song oil, Coins in a Fountain incense, a golden earring, an emerald-green ribbon, and a gold coin.

INSTRUCTIONS   Anoint the candle with Mermaid's Song oil. Light the candle and the incense. Place the gold earring on your ear. Tie the green ribbon in a bow around your left ankle. Place the gold coin in one of your shoes. Recite the incantation facing south. Do this ritual every day of the waxing moon during the Jupiter hour. Do not perform this spell when the moon is waning.

If this spell is performed for three consecutive moons, your prosperity will begin to flow.

INCANTATION

> Pirate, Pirate in disguise,
> Bring thy gains before my eyes.
> Bounty of the emerald satin,
> Around thy foothold in bow-like fashion.
> The golden coin within thy shoe,
> Will ten times ten when worn by you.
> Thy ear adorned with gold and shine,
> Will light the path to the mine.
> Blessed by Jupiter when moon is half,
> All will increase while it doeth wax.
> But when the moon is in its wane,
> Hide the gold and ribbon the same.
> Three times three under the stars,
> Thy fortune will come with force of Mars.
> Pirate, Pirate, passage is due,
> Deliver the bounty of the golden shoe.
> So Mote It Be.

To Obtain an Extra $100

The Money Nest

TIME   Waxing Thursday, Jupiter hour.

TOOLS   A green candle, Mermaid's Song oil, Lucky Hand incense, material with which to build a nest (i.e., straw, hair, grass, twigs, etc.), one crow's feather, one blade of green grass, and a nearby tree to place the nest in.

INSTRUCTIONS   Anoint the green candle with Mermaid's Song oil. Light the candle and the incense. Create a nest out of natural things that a bird would use. Place the crow's feather and the one blade of grass inside the nest. Recite the incantation while smudging with the incense and turning the nest deosil. Place the nest in a well-protected area of the tree. Recite the incantation once more while turning yourself deosil three times. Check the nest every morning for any moisture. When the nest is completely wet with either dew or rain, your money will come.

INCANTATION

> *Needle of grass,*
> *Feather of crow.*
> *Deosil will turn,*
> *And money will grow.*
> *Angels in heaven,*
> *Hear my request.*
> *Shower me money,*
> *Into this nest,*
> *Raphael in Eastern sky,*
> *Rain prosperity where 'tis dry.*
> *Increase the moneys that are few,*
> *And fill my nest with your dew.*
> *So Mote It Be.*

To Get a Loan

Lender Be

TIME   Waxing Thursday, Jupiter hour.

TOOLS   One green candle, Jade oil, Emerald incense, a green ink pen, a seven-inch swatch of white muslin, a new dollar bill, and seven pine needles.

INSTRUCTIONS   Anoint the green candle with Jade oil. Light the candle and the incense. With the green pen, draw a pentagram upon the muslin. Do not put a circle around the pentagram. Visualize a check being placed in your hands in the amount you are requesting. Place the seven pine needles in the center of the muslin. Fold the muslin into fourths. Recite the incantation. This is now your talisman. Place it in your Book of Shadows or Grimoire where you have this spell written. (This spell works really well for re-financing or for loans on housing or cars.) Keep the talisman there until your loan is approved. Place the dollar bill to mark your page. It brings good vibrations.

INCANTATION

> *I conjure thee talisman of green,*
> *Grant me money from Jupiter's queen.*
> *Powers of the Earth and Heaven,*
> *I offer thee needles of seven.*
> *Folded in cloth of ancient estate,*
> *Quartered be placed into my fate.*
> *Into the Shadows of Wiccan's wise,*
> *Lend me the moneys of my prize.*
> *So Mote It Be.*

To Have Abundance of Wealth in and Around Your Home

Planting Prosperity

TIME   Full Moon, Jupiter hour.

TOOLS   One green candle, Bayberry oil, Prosperity incense, a four-by-five-foot planting space near the front door of your home (it needs to be very sunny), rich planting soil, five pots of marigold starters, seventy marigold seeds, a healthy aloe vera plant, and one gallon of holy water.

INSTRUCTIONS Anoint the candle with Bayberry oil. Prepare the planting area near your front door. Dig the dirt and add the rich planting soil so it is abundant with nutrients. Plant the five marigold starters in a star configuration. Add the seeds to fill in the lines for the star (twelve seeds to each line). Take only a piece of the aloe vera and squeeze its juice on each of the five plants. Place the green candle and the incense in the center of your star, and light them. Add the holy water to your new flowers. If they need more than the one gallon of holy water, you can add tap water. Recite the incantation. Let the candle and the incense burn for the entire Jupiter hour. Every waxing Thursday, light the green candle and incense and recite the incantation to keep your prosperity coming.

INCANTATION

As the sun will rise, the sun will set,
Gather seeds of marigolds at their best.
Milk the "juice of bounty" from aloes dry,
To free the magick and watch it fly.
Feel the power, breathe the air,
Wealth and prosperity will soon be there.
Jupiter watches on the day of the round,
To ensure expansion to be homeward bound.
Prosperity is planted and blessed with flow,
Wealth is welcomed and poverty must go.
So Mote It Be.

8

SPELLS THAT ARE *Purple*

Thirteen Witches stir the pot,
Lavender, violets, forget-me-nots.
Brewing for power and psychic force,
Emulating the Goddess source.
—Belladonna

The color purple represents magick involving power of all kinds, control over others, psychic energy, wisdom, intuition, influence, confidence, royalty, and heavenly guides.

TO DIVINE YOUR FUTURE HUSBAND

Fifty-two Steps

TIME Full Moon, Moon hour.

TOOLS One purple candle, Marriage Mind oil, and Oracle incense.

INSTRUCTIONS   This spell is to be done in the mountains or in a wooded area. Anoint the purple candle with Marriage Mind oil and light it. Burn the incense and meditate to the Goddess for accurate and skilled divining. Go to the wooded area and start your journey. Perform the spell while reciting it and doing as it says.

INCANTATION

> *Walk through the garden of the Goddess Divine,*
> *If looking for a husband, answers you'll find.*
> *Take fifty-two steps north as your*
>   *journey begins,*
> *Have faith and courage, on you it depends.*
> *Stop and look to the left, then to the right,*
> *This is where you will spot a single source of life.*
> *If none is to be seen, then no reason to remain,*
> *Forget your journey, go back from*
>   *where you came.*
> *If life you see, then go on if you dare,*
> *Take fifty-two steps more, a bird awaits there.*
> *The color of the bird, whether he sits or flies,*
> *Will reveal the color of your husband's eyes.*
> *Be happy, be thrilled, your answer shown,*
> *Take fifty-two steps more and find the stone.*
> *Look about the rocks that are scattered there,*
> *The one you touch is the color of his hair.*
> *Walk fifty-two steps more, the final steps to be,*
> *Extend your left hand outward and*
>   *there stands a tree.*
> *Strong, weak, short, or tall,*
> *This is the size of your man in his all.*
> *Your journey now over, but your search begins,*
> *Look for your husband, your mate, your friend.*
> *So Mote It Be.*

To Initiate a New Coven

The Coven's Blood

TIME   The first part is to be done during the Full Moon, Moon hour; the second part is to be done exactly thirty days past, Moon hour.

TOOLS   A purple candle, Magick oil, Wiccan incense, snips of hair and nails from each participating Witch, a red mojo, nettle, sage, sweetpea, nutmeg, star anise, yellow flower petals, and lavender.

INSTRUCTIONS   Do this during the Full Moon at the Moon hour. Anoint the candle with Magick oil. Light the candle and the incense. Snip the hair and nails of each Witch and place them in the red mojo. Place all the herbs and flowers together in a bowl and place it on the altar. Leave all ingredients undisturbed for thirty days.

Thirty days later, light the candle and incense. Place all herbs in the mojo and add three drops of Magick oil. Pass the mojo to each Witch as she or he recites her or his Wiccan name. Recite the incantation.

Have the mojo present each time the coven convenes. This seals the coven to be as one from this day forward.

INCANTATION

For no less than thirty, this energy has sat,
The Moon has waned and the Moon has waxed.
With trust and honor this coven has formed,
Gather hair and nails that have been shorn.
Presented for blessing, the lot has been cast,
Alpha and Omega, from beginning to last.
We brew thee nettle and a pinch of sage,
To give protection and wisdom of age.
Sweetpea and nutmeg will carry us through,
With friendships bonded and prosperity, too.
The star of anise will weave and tie,

Boost the psyche and open the Eye.
The petals of gold from a flower or bud,
Will grow good health in the coven's blood.
The seed of lavender will add the power,
To build foundation in the mighty tower.
Nine plus one will give us ten,
The oil of Magick will now transcend.
One thing more and more is done,
The Wiccan name of everyone.
Sealed eternally in the scarlet flannel,
Placed before the Wiccan mantle.
Together we stand in a circle bound,
Uniting in power to draw the moon down.
So Mote It Be!

To Divine an Answer

Pebble Peering

Time   Hare Moon, Mercury hour.

Tools   A purple candle, Oracle oil and incense, small pebbles, and a calm lake.

Instructions   Go to a secluded lake and find an area that has small, flat stones. Anoint the candle with Oracle oil. Light the candle and the incense. Meditate and center yourself. Call upon the Goddess to answer your questions through the pebbles. Recite the incantation. Skip the stones across the lake. The even and odd numbers of skips will reveal the answers.

Incantation

Half the lunar lights the sky,
Reveal the truth in reply.
I ask for answers in the stones I throw,

Even number is yes, the odd is no.
So Mote It Be.

To Divine if Your Lover's Intentions Are True

Call Upon the Dead

TIME   Part one is to be completed on a waxing Friday, Mercury hour; part two is to be completed on a Full Moon.

TOOLS   One small purple candle, one small pink candle, High John the Conqueror oil, Oracle incense, hibiscus, pinches of roses, violets, dandelions, celery seed, witch's grass, and a red mojo.

INSTRUCTIONS   Anoint both candles with the oil. Light both candles and the incense. Place all the herbs inside the mojo and anoint it with the oil. Recite the incantation.

On the day or night of the full moon, place the mojo on a grave you have selected. Go back to the grave the next day or night at the exact same hour. If the mojo has disappeared, then his love is false. If the mojo has moved to another grave, then he loves someone else. If the mojo is exactly where you left it, then his love is true. Retrieve the mojo and bury it near your home.

INCANTATION

Family of the Goddess divine,
Tell me if my love is blind.
Show me what my love desires,
So I may know his inner fire.
If his love is true, then I shall wait,
To retrieve this magickal bag of fate.
If his love is false, then in its stead,
Shall be no gift on the grave of the dead.
If by chance magick moves this tool,
To another's grave, then I am the fool.

> *For this will tell that he loves another,*
> *I will not break and I will not shudder.*
> *I ask for truth in this garden of souls,*
> *For better, for worse, it is the toll.*
> *Rounded beacon, light up the sky,*
> *Divine the future for my lover and I.*
> *So Mote It Be.*

TO GAIN POSITIVE CONTROL OVER SOMEONE

The Sword and the Stone

TIME   Full Moon, Moon Hour.

TOOLS   One purple candle, Do As I Say oil, Controlling incense, a picture of the person you wish to control, an amethyst, a small castle (I built a great castle with my child's Legos), a picture of yourself, and an athame.

INSTRUCTIONS   Anoint the candle with the oil. Light the candle and the incense. Pass the picture widdershins through the incense smoke. Put the picture on a flat surface and the amethyst stone over the person's face. Place the castle over the picture and the stone. Place the picture of you on top of the castle so your picture will shadow the other picture at all times. With the athame, draw three deosil circles around the whole spell and recite the incantation.

This spell will work for a maximum of seventy-two hours. Disassemble the whole spell to release it.

INCANTATION

> *By power of Moon and athame,*
> *Precedence I wish to gain.*
> *The entire dominion is totally mine,*
> *Your every move is now confined.*
> *Within my castle you are bound,*

Until I release you from this ground.
Do as I want, do as I say,
I am master, you are slave.
Remain inferior by shadows of me,
This is my will, So Mote It Be.

For Intense Psychic Abilities

The Buchu Bowl

TIME   Waxing Wednesday, Moon Hour.

TOOLS   One purple candle, Moon oil, Psychic incense, buchu, onion, lemongrass, yarrow, warm water, and an earthen bowl.

INSTRUCTIONS   Anoint the candle with the oil. Light the candle and the incense. Pray to the Goddess to obtain a substantial increase in your psychic power. Steep the herbs in warm water in the bowl. Strain the herbs and recite the incantation. Drink the infusion right from the bowl. An increase in psychic abilities will be instantaneous.

INCANTATION

Mercury waxing sky.
Moon opens Eye.
Buchu in the bowl,
Infusion enters soul.
Window opens truth,
Sayer is the Sooth.
So Mote It Be.

To Divine Your Future Mate

The Man in the Mirror

TIME   Waxing phase, Venus hour.

TOOLS   A pink candle, Lover's oil, Moon incense, one red apple, one hairbrush, one hand mirror, and one standing mirror.

INSTRUCTIONS Anoint the candle with Lover's oil. Light the candle and the incense. Place the apple in the center of your altar; place the hairbrush on the right and the hand mirror on the left. The standing mirror should be behind the diviner.

Recite the incantation. Stroke your hair three times with the hairbrush, bite the apple, and pick up the mirror and look over your shoulder. In the hand mirror you will see the face of the person you are going to marry.

INCANTATION

> *Thrice the hair is stroked,*
> *The skin of the apple is broke.*
> *The glass reveals the fate,*
> *With the face of my future mate.*
> *So Mote It Be.*

TO MAKE A LONG-STAYING VISITOR WANT TO LEAVE YOUR HOME

Take Leave

TIME Waning Tuesday, Mars hour.

TOOLS One purple candle, Widdershins oil, Do As I Say incense, a mortar and pestle, thirteen blueberries, one cup of graveyard dirt, six pinches of calamus, and one pinch of garlic.

INSTRUCTIONS Anoint the candle with Widdershins oil. Light the candle and the incense. With the mortar and pestle, grind together the blueberries, graveyard dirt, calamus, and garlic. Suffumigate the potion thirteen times in widdershins motion. Visualize the visitor leaving your home on the date you want him or her to leave. Recite the incantation over the potion. Place three pinches of the potion beneath the mattress of where the visitor is sleeping. Divide the remaining potion into two and place equal amounts beneath the welcome mat at your front and back doors. Your visitor will have the urge to flee from you very soon. Don't forget to remove the potion after your visitor has left from the sleeping area and both welcome mats—or no one will ever want to come to your home.

INCANTATION

Visitor, friend, lengthy guest,
Energy now sweeps you west.
End of talk, end of stay,
Now you must be on your way.
Clock is ticking; the date has come,
Pack your bags and now you'll run.
Out of my home, you must flee,
With harm to none, So Mote It Be.

TO RECEIVE PROPHETIC ANSWERS BY WAY OF YOUR DREAMS

Now I Lay Me Down to Dream

TIME   Any day, any moon phase, Moon hour.

TOOLS   One large purple candle, Psychic oil, Beneficial Dream incense, a pinch of cinnamon, a pinch of powdered aloe, a pinch of dragon's blood, and a mortar and pestle.

INSTRUCTIONS   Anoint the candle with Psychic oil. Light the candle and the incense. Place the aloe, dragon's blood, and cinnamon in the mortar and pestle and grind it to a fine powder. As the incense is burning, slowly add the mixture. Recite the incantation. Before you go to sleep, invite the Angels into your sleep chamber. Tell the Angels what it is you would like to know and ask them to aid you and to protect you in your dreams and in your life.

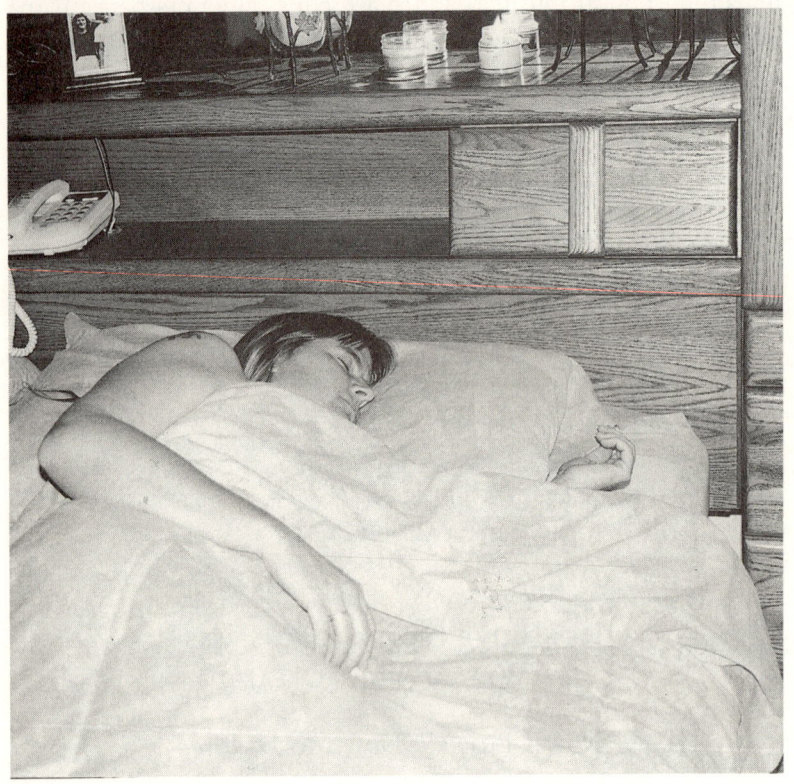

Divining through dreams

Incantation

>   *Divining wisdom I now invoke,*
>   *Open the channels with gifted smoke.*
>   *Angels deliver me to the place,*
>   *Of intuitive minds and gentle grace.*
>   *Grant me vision,*
>   *Grant me sight,*
>   *The door of dreams,*
>   *Opens my sight.*
>   *So Mote It Be.*

To Prevent Someone From Being Accident-Prone

Bend Me, Shake Me, Any Way You Want To

TIME   Waning Tuesday, Sun hour.

TOOLS   One purple candle, Protection oil, Do As I Say incense, seven blue pipe cleaners, and two small pillows.

INSTRUCTIONS   Anoint the candle with Protection oil. Light the candle and the incense. Arrange the pipe cleaners to resemble the person who needs the protection, kind of like a "poppet." Suffumigate it seven times in deosil motion. Recite the incantation. Place

Poppets used for protection

the poppet between two pillows as you would to protect someone from accidents. Keep it there for as long as you feel the person is accident-prone. This spell lasts for about ten days. If someone is in need of longer protection, repeat the spell.

INCANTATION

I am in control of all that you do,
Caution and safety are now with you.
Feathery pillows in towers tall,
Prevent the accidents of slip and fall.
Blessings be with you and in your shoes,
Keep you safe from scrapes and bruise.
For I am in control of your very being,
Safety assured is what I am seeing.
So Mote It Be.

TO COMMUNICATE WITH A SPECIFIC PERSON WHO IS DECEASED

Eyes Wide Shut

TIME   Full Moon, Mercury hour.

TOOLS   Two tablespoons of bugleweed, two tablespoons of calendula, a mortar and pestle, one purple candle, All Hallows oil, and Oracle incense.

INSTRUCTIONS   Grind together the bugleweed and calendula in the mortar and pestle. It does not have to be fine as powder, but it does need to be well mixed. Take the herbs, candle, oil, and incense with you and go to the graveside of the person you would like to communicate with. Anoint the candle with All Hallows oil. Light the candle and the incense. Sprinkle only half of the mixed herbs over the body area of the deceased person. Keep the other half with you. Lie over the body area of the person and recite incantation 1. When you return to your home, place the remaining herbs beneath your mattress in the same fashion as you did at the graveyard. Recite incantation 2 and go to sleep. The dead shall communicate with you in your dreams.

INCANTATION 1

> *I gently waken this resting spirit,*
> *Listen to my voice and do not fear it.*
> *I wish to talk to your heart,*
> *I ask for distance to no longer part.*
> *I lay upon this hallowed ground,*
> *To join our energy within the round.*
> *Embrace this light as it beams,*
> *Come tonight within my dreams.*
> *So Mote It Be.*

INCANTATION 2

> *Power of herbs and voice of dead,*
> *Open the visions beneath this bed.*
> *Veil release and words commence,*
> *Spirits of peace, end my suspense.*
> *My mind will rest and dreams will come,*
> *Your presence is blessed as we become one.*
> *Sanctity herbs and the dead will speak,*
> *Satisfy what I do seek.*
> *So Mote It Be.*

9

SPELLS THAT ARE *Gold*

Embrace the dreams that I caress,
Golden emeralds achieve success.
Warming amber dawns the day,
Wisdom is what I ask and pray.
—Belladonna

The color gold represents magick involving fortune, success in any endeavor, higher-than-middle-class living, proprietorship, accomplishment, reverence, and extended energy.

To Promote Success in Life

Ten Pennies for Success

TIME   Full Moon, Moon Hour.

TOOLS   One gold candle, Cleomay oil, Success incense, and ten copper pennies.

INSTRUCTIONS   Anoint the candle with Cleomay oil. Light the candle and the incense. Take the candle, incense, and pennies outside of your home. Hold the pennies in your right hand and face north.

Take a step to the right and toss a penny over your right shoulder while reciting the appropriate incantation. Repeat this until all the pennies have been used; then return to your home without looking back at where you have been.

INCANTATION 1   *I am successful.*

INCANTATION 2   *I am successful in what I think and feel.*

INCANTATION 3   *I am successful in all that I hear and speak.*

INCANTATION 4   *I am successful in reaching my goals.*

INCANTATION 5   *I am successful in love and happiness.*

INCANTATION 6   *I am successful in all that I desire.*

INCANTATION 7   *I am attracting successful people to me.*

INCANTATION 8   *I am successful in all areas of health.*

INCANTATION 9   *I am successful in my home and work areas.*

INCANTATION 10   *I am a success because I am a creation of the Goddess and the God. This is my will, So Mote It Be.*

TO BRING SUCCESS

Horsepower

TIME   Waxing Sunday, Sun hour.

TOOLS   One gold candle, Midas oil, Myrrh incense, rich potting soil, a green flowerpot, a magnetic horseshoe, one gold coin, honeysuckle seedlings, and water.

INSTRUCTIONS   Anoint the candle with Midas oil. Light the candle and the incense. Place the potting soil in the base of the pot. Place the magnetic horseshoe in the pot. Add more potting soil and place the gold coin on top. Add more potting soil and plant the honeysuckle seedlings. Add the final layer of potting soil and give it water. Recite the incantation.

Place the plant in a very sunny, warm area and let the honeysuckle grow for a minimum of seventy days. After that time, uproot one third of them and feed it to a horse. If the horse eats it, your success is assured. If the horse refuses it, grow the remaining honeysuckle another seventy days and try again.

INCANTATION

Magnet horseshoe, magnet gold,
Deliver success to me tenfold.
Honeysuckle rich and sweet,
Success to come when horses eat.
Power the soil, suckle the honey,
Bring to me abundant money.
Seventy days to reinforce,
Success ingested by the horse.
So Mote It Be.

TO ACHIEVE A PERSONAL GOAL

Seven Gold Rings

TIME   Waxing Sunday, Jupiter hour.

TOOLS   One gold candle, Amber oil, Isis incense, purple parchment, black ink, and seven gold rings.

INSTRUCTIONS   Keep in mind that achievements are not material possessions. Anoint the candle with Amber oil. Light the candle and the incense. Visualize what it is you would like to achieve. On the purple parchment, write in black ink exactly what it is and when you would like to achieve it. Roll the parchment into a scroll and place seven gold rings around it. Pass the scroll and rings through the incense smoke and recite the incantation.

Place the scroll and rings beneath your bed. Pray to the Goddess every night that your goal be achieved in a timely manner. When you have achieved your goal, burn the parchment and feel free to wear your gold rings any time.

INCANTATION

Upon the parchment inscribed in black,
Special achievement in which I lack.
Scroll is bound by seven gold rings,
Fumed by amber as it swings.
Beneath my chamber it shall stay,
To the Goddess I shall pray.
Rings be bound till I achieve,
All that I am to receive.
So Mote It Be.

To Be Discovered for Your Talents

Star Gazing

TIME   Hare Moon, Venus hour.

TOOLS   This spell works very well if your ambition is to be a singer or actor. One large gold candle, one orange candle, Myrrh oil, Isis incense, three coffee beans, one teaspoon of honey, one teaspoon of sugar, one teaspoon of lavender, one teaspoon of cinnamon, a mortar and pestle, seven ounces of consecrated water, one peacock feather, a pen with gold ink, and a publicity-type photo of yourself.

INSTRUCTIONS   Anoint both the gold and orange candles with Myrrh oil. Light the candles and the incense. Place the herbs and spices in the mortar and grind them into a fine powder with the pestle. Boil the seven ounces of water and combine the powder with the water. Stir the mixture deosil seven times with the peacock feather. With the gold pen, draw pentagrams upon the photo with special attention to the lips and hands. Pass the photo through the steam of the brew.

Allow a few minutes for the brew to cool. Recite the incantation and drink the brew while visualizing your talents being discovered. Your name will soon be spoken by influential people.

INCANTATION

Unseen moon with power to wax,
Wary the populace it attracts.
Propel the wind with magickal force,
Take my name to its source.
Within this brew I will taste,
Success calling me in haste.
Smoke unfurling upon my lips,
Stars and pentacles at fingertips.
Within this moment, I compel,
Only those who make me excel.
Recognition of my name,
Draws the future of my fame.
So Mote It Be.

To Sell a Successful Business

Wholesale Business

TIME   Waxing Sunday, Jupiter hour.

TOOLS   One gold candle, one green candle, one orange candle, Money Drawing oil, Midas incense, play money in the amount you are asking for your business, a pen with green ink, one piece of green parchment, two tablespoons of cinquefoil, one whole star anise, a pinch of dock, a dash of orange bergamot, five spearmint leaves, one teaspoon of fenugreek, a pinch of heliotrope, three pinches of sugar, a gallon of water, and an earthen pot.

INSTRUCTIONS   This spell works best if you ask a reasonable price and market your business well. Anoint all three candles with Money Drawing oil. Light the candles and the incense. Place all of the play money beneath the gold candle. With the pen, write the name of your business, the complete address, and the phone number on the green parchment, and place it beneath the green candle.

Place all the herbs and the water in the pot. Steep the herbs for exactly three minutes.

While holding the orange candle, recite the incantation over the mixture. Sprinkle the entire mixture deosil around the inside and outside of the place of business. Light the three candles each and every day until the business is under contract to be sold.

INCANTATION

> Buyer, Buyer, Business transpire,
> Seek position that you desire.
> Bring me cash for business to sell,
> Bless your days with profits well.
> Solution, infusion, business transfusion,
> Bring me buyer for final conclusion.
> Contract signed and deed be done,
> Cash and gold become as one.
> Witch to stitch the final hitch,
> Sprinkle the potion to make us rich.
> Hasten the steps to business door,
> Exchange me cash and buy my store.
> So Mote It Be.

To Extend the Life of Mechanical Devices

The Egyptian Energy Extender

TIME   Any waxing day, Mercury hour.

TOOLS   One gold candle, Pharaoh oil, Sweet Clover incense, a crystal pyramid, and a pendulum.

INSTRUCTIONS   This spell works well on all modes of transportation, washers and dryers, refrigerators, and all large machines. But be sure you cast it before the machine dies completely! Anoint the candle with the oil. Light the candle and the incense. Place the crystal pyramid on top of the mechanical device. Hold the pendulum over the pyramid and recite the incantation. Check the pendulum: If it swings clockwise, the spell has been received. If the pendulum swings counter-clockwise, the machine has no life force left.

INCANTATION

> Within the power of the crystal,
> Life extends like a thistle.
> Project your force and intervene,
> Breathe new life in my machine.
> So Mote It Be.

To Improve the Memory

Memory Banks

TIME   Full Moon, Moon hour.

TOOLS   One gold candle, Van Van oil, Memory incense, a pen with gold ink, yellow parchment, a small bank in the shape of a person, and thirteen pennies.

INSTRUCTIONS   Anoint the candle with the oil. Light the candle and the incense. Anoint your third eye with the oil.

With the pen, write the words "Retain the knowledge. Reveal it now." on the parchment. Anoint the parchment with the oil and pass it through the incense smoke. Fold the parchment into a triangle and place it in the bottom of the bank.

Recite the incantation and with each verse, drop a penny into the bank. When you need to remember something important, make a mental commitment to remember it and place a penny into the bank to hold it there. When you need to remember it, simply pick up the piggy bank and shake it to jar your memory.

INCANTATION

> Copper coin in the bank,
> My memory is no longer blank.
>
> Shiny Lincoln, shiny penny,
> My gifts from God are so many.
>
> I will see and remember,
> From January to December.
>
> Tokens are a tiny key,
> To unlock my memory.
>
> Tails are no, heads are yes,
> No longer will I have to guess.
>
> Facts are bright and always clear,
> When I smile from ear to ear.
>
> Retain the knowledge, reveal it now,
> Anoint third eye between the brow.
>
> Make the coins jingle and clank,
> As I jog my memory bank.
>
> Strong and sharp is my mind,
> When I search, I will find.
>
> Thank you, Goddess for the gift
> Of making my mind extremely swift.
>
> Increase my coins by the number,
> Prevent my mind from needless slumber.
>
> I am smart and I am rich,
> I am a totally awesome witch.

Raphael will bless me well,
Forever with my memory spell.
So Mote It Be.

Gargoyle banking

To Make Someone Accept a Business Proposal That Would Be Good for Him or Her and for You

B.B.S.

Time   Waning Sunday, Sun hour.

Tools   One gold candle, Huntress oil, Sweet Clover incense, a very small portion of your own blood that has been lost naturally and without invasion to the body, (menstrual blood works well), a teaspoon of basil, a teaspoon of Solomon's Seal, an earthen bowl, and one large amethyst stone.

Instructions   Anoint the candle with Huntress oil. Light the candle and the incense. Place the blood, basil, and Solomon's Seal in an earthen bowl and mix well. Recite the incantation over the mixture. Place all of these ingredients in a sacred outdoor area or outdoor altar. Secure the contents with the large amethyst stone by placing it in the earthen bowl, so the ingredients will not be blown away. Place a pinch of incense near this mixture and light it again. Recite the incantation again. After the spell has worked, come back to the area and remove only the bowl and the amethyst. Most of the mixture should be gone by natural means. Scatter the remaining mixture to the earth.

Incantation

> *Basil, Blood, and Seal,*
> *Spin the business wheel.*
> *Sign the contract and deal is done,*
> *Today is mine and I have won.*
> *No more delays, your call must come,*
> *Today is mine and I have won.*
> *Bless this business by moon and sun,*
> *Today is mine and business is done.*
> *Basil, Blood, and Seal,*
> *Grant me this business deal.*
> *So Mote It Be.*

To Find Something That Is Lost

The Treasure Hunt

TIME   Waxing Monday, Mercury Hour.

TOOLS   One gold candle, Psychic oil, Isis incense, a rough draft or map of your home or office (wherever you lost your treasure), and a musical triangle.

INSTRUCTIONS   Anoint the candle with the oil. Light the candle and the incense. During meditation, ask the Angels to help you locate your lost item. Lay your map flat on the floor. Ask the Angels to tell you where it is by the sound of the ping of the triangle when

Create a map to find lost items.

you strike it. Recite the incantation. Ask the Angels to make the sound be totally different when you have reached the place on the map where the treasure is located. You can actually take the triangle with you to the room and ask where in the room the lost item is. Let the Angels lead you, and remember to thank Them when you have found it.

INCANTATION

> I call upon Angels of absent treasure,
> Reveal to me by musical measure.
> Allow the sound befall my ear,
> Make the music draw me near.
> Upon the map I draw the site,
> Of where my treasure lies tonight.
> Lead me to the depths of pitch,
> Treasures abound this baffled Witch.
> So Mote It Be.

TO OBTAIN YOUR DAILY GOALS

The Goalie

TIME   Lunar eclipse, any hour.

TOOLS   Four gold candles, Wolf's Song oil, Cleomay incense, your daily agenda, calendar, or whatever you use to write your daily goals on, and your Wiccan broom.

INSTRUCTIONS   Anoint the gold candles with Wolf's Song oil. Light the candles and the incense. Place your agenda in the center of the four candles. As the moon is eclipsing, take your broom to sweep away all obstacles that prevent you from reaching your daily goals. Remember to sweep away from the agenda, not toward it. Recite the incantation as you do this. The power of the eclipse will reverse the negative energy to be positive energy, and it will allow you to accomplish your daily goals. The spell will be complete after the first rainfall comes.

INCANTATION

> *Luna, Luna, passing Sun,*
> *Reverse the curse of aimless run.*
> *Remove the walls that bound my shame,*
> *Thunder, blunder, let it rain!*
> *Luna, Luna, passing Moon,*
> *Eclipse the night and the noon.*
> *Sweep away the holds that bar,*
> *Shine with gold the brilliant star.*
> *So Mote It Be.*

Use magick on your agenda to stay focused and on track toward your goals.

To Have Success That Is Blessed by the Gods

Gold Fingers

TIME   Full Moon, Jupiter hour.

TOOLS   One gold candle, Midas oil, Helping Hand incense, one perfectly shaped lucky hand root, a small amount of melted gold (not imitation), a fourteen-inch gold necklace, and any apparatus necessary to connect the lucky hand to the necklace. Any accessory to this charm must be made of gold.

INSTRUCTIONS   Anoint the candle with Midas oil. Light the candle and the incense. Dip the lucky hand root into the melted gold. After the gold has dried onto the root, suffumigate the hand fourteen times in deosil. Recite the incantation while suffumigating. The necklace and the attachment can be put together anytime. Wear the gold lucky hand on the necklace any time you desire Divine intervention. Simply hold the golden hand with your hand and pray to the Goddess and God to be with you.

INCANTATION

> *Gold that lays upon this hand,*
> *Mineral and herb of earthen land.*
> *Divine the charm upon my wear,*
> *Be with me in urgent prayer.*
> *I call upon Your blessed name,*
> *To aid me in the quest I claim.*
> *Guide me with a path of wise,*
> *Open the doors and my eyes.*
> *So Mote It Be.*

To Remove All Obstacles That May Keep Success From Happening

Blowin' in the Wind

TIME   Waning Sunday, Mars hour.

TIME   One gold candle, Golden Emerald oil, Pharaoh incense, a nail, seven bills of play currency ranging from ones to twenties, and a seven-inch green or gold string.

Turn play currency into real money with magick.

INSTRUCTIONS   Anoint the gold candle with Golden Emerald oil. Light the candle and the incense. Write on the reverse side of the currency exactly what you want to be removed. Place a hole in each of the play currency. Run the string through the hole and tie a knot. Suffumigate the currency in the incense four times deosil. Recite the incantation. Hang the string of currency on a nail outside your home. Allow the wind magick to carry away all of your obstacles and blow in success.

INCANTATION

Cast this spell into the wind,
Response to fly and transcend.
Deals of money now to flow,
Accept the offer as it blows.
Remove all obstacles in my way,
Make success without delay.
Take the contracts now and seize,
Cash will flow in the breeze.
So Mote It Be.

10

SPELLS THAT ARE *Brown*

> Around the hearthside holding hands,
> Draped in browns, beige, and tan.
> A family gathers to honor their home,
> Bound by Witches, Priestess, and Crone.
> —Belladonna

The color brown represents magick involving marriage, partnerships, unions, hearth and home, children, stable friendships, animals in general, bonded energy, and relatives.

TO KEEP YOUR BELOVED MALE AT HOME

Magnet the Man

TIME   Waxing Friday, Sun hour.

TOOLS   One brown candle, Ravenwood oil, Stay at Home incense, a picture of the two of you together, one magnet, endive, and a juicy steak.

INSTRUCTIONS   Anoint the candle with Ravenwood oil. Light the candle and the incense. Glue the picture of the two of you on the magnet. Pass this deosil through the incense smoke. Do the same thing with the endive. Cook the steak and serve it on top of the endive. Recite the incantation before you give it to him.

At dinner, bring up the subject of how much you enjoy him being home with you. Make him admit how much he loves it. As he cuts the steak, he is cutting away any urge to leave home.

INCANTATION

> *Magnet my man to his loving home,*
> *Release all cravings to ever roam.*
> *Bound him ever with love and desire,*
> *May only my presence light his fire.*
> *Cut away the nonsense and the toy,*
> *Build my man and release the boy.*
> *Observe our faces and bond our hearts,*
> *Never once yearning to be apart.*
> *So Mote It Be.*

To Promote Happiness in the Home

Hearth and Home

TIME   Waxing Sunday, Sun hour.

TOOLS   One brown candle, Hearthside oil, Ravenwood incense, lavender, witch's grass, a small lock of gray hair from a woman who has had children, a cauldron, a secret wish that each family member has written on a piece of paper, and a lump of coal.

INSTRUCTIONS   Anoint the candle with Hearthside oil. Light the candle and the incense. Visualize each member of your household smiling and feeling happy. Place the lavender, witch's grass, and lock of hair in the cauldron. Place the paper wishes on top of the herbs and hair. Place the coal on top of the wishes. Anoint the coal with Hearthside oil. Recite the incantation. Ignite the coal, wishes, hair, and herbs and allow them to burn to ashes.

When the ashes have cooled, tell each family member to go outside and face east. Each member should take a pinch of ashes and throw it over her or his left shoulder while visualizing her or his wish. The remaining ashes should be spread around the base of a tree.

INCANTATION

Within the cauldron dwells a mass,
Of coal, lavender, witch's grass.
Gleaming steel of matron hair,
Dispels sadness and solitaire.
Anointed with home and hearth,
Lit by candle sable and dark.
Recite them all, "Happy are we,"
Wishes burned in harmony.
Ashes cooled and facing east,
Left shoulder tossed and released.
The tree shall house all the rest,
For all be happy and very blessed.
So Mote It Be.

FOR COUPLES HAVING BAD LUCK IN THEIR MARRIAGE

The Wedding Eclipse

TIME   One week prior to your anniversary date, Saturn hour.

TOOLS   One white candle, one pink candle, one gray candle, Handfast oil, Blessed Be incense, holy water, an altar with all the tools, a copy of the marriage license, a picture from your wedding day, and your wedding rings.

INSTRUCTIONS   This spell is best suited for people married an odd number of years, and not to be used at all if married less than seven years. This spell is like a divorce followed by a wedding. It will give the married couple a better chance at success for the rest of their years together. Anoint all candles with Handfast oil. Light all candles and incense. The couple must perform this ceremony in total privacy. They both should be wearing white garments or nothing at all. The wedding rings may have a negative attachment to them, and this needs to be discussed. The old rings may be purified and rededicated; the purchase of new ones is a good alternative. In either case, the rings need to be consecrated and purified.

Anoint each other on the forehead with holy water in the sign of the cross. Say a silent prayer asking for forgiveness and cleansing. With the Handfast oil, anoint each other's ring fingers. Kiss each other's hands.

Recite the incantation together. Each person should hold a corner of the marriage license; burn it with the flame of the gray candle, then burn the wedding picture with the flame of the pink candle.

The ashes of the incense and burned items are to be buried outside under a fruit tree. The couple recites the incantation again over the buried items. They kiss one another in brotherly fashion.

For one solid week until the anniversary date, the couple must stay clear of each other. They speak only when they have to and are not to be intimate in any way. This is the time to reflect about the mistakes that have been made by both partners. Use this time to forgive and cleanse. No bad memories or unforgiven issues are allowed to be in your head again. You are clean and absolved. This ritual is followed by the Handfast After the Eclipse Ritual, to be performed on the date of your anniversary.

INCANTATION

The eclipse of our marriage has come,
The moon has clouded the sun.
No joy or bliss remains,

The smiles have turned to pain.
Our past is gone and erased,
Old wounds are no longer faced.
Forgiveness fills our hearts,
Balance will be the start.
We dissolve and divorce our past,
Our ending is here at last.
Seven days pass to cleanse,
Our hearts have made amends.
United with love and passion,
Remarried in Handfast fashion.
Goddess and God will only bless,
The love we will confess.
The pain and selfishness that we bury,
Will never occur after we marry.
Love begins with a heart that's free,
This is our will, So Mote It Be.

TO UNITE IN MARRIAGE

The Handfast After the Eclipse

TIME The first part is to be performed one day prior to the anniversary date at the Venus hour; the second part should be done on the anniversary date, Venus hour.

TOOLS A gray candle, a pink candle, Blessed Be oil, Handfast incense, a piece of gray parchment, a piece of pink parchment, a red apple, and three white candles.

INSTRUCTIONS For the first part of this ritual, anoint the gray and pink candles with Blessed Be oil. Light both candles and the incense.

On the piece of gray parchment, write all of the things you personally disliked about the marriage. Be specific. On the piece of pink parchment, write all of the things you love about each other. Again, be specific. Sit down and read each other the gray list first. There is to be no discussion or comments. Then read each other the pink list. Again, there is to be no discussion. Together, anoint the gray parchment and burn it by the flame of the gray candle. The couple kisses, and then each takes one bite from the red apple. They take the remaining apple and the pink parchment outside and bury it near a fruit tree. They kiss.

The rest of the day should be spent planning their goals for the future.

The second part of the ceremony takes place outside. On the ground, draw a large circle and divide it in half. Each person stands in one half. The couple should not wear the same clothes they were married in, or the same clothes they wore in the Wedding Eclipse. They should either do this skyclad or in new clothes that are all white.

Anoint the three white candles with Blessed Be oil. Light the candles and the incense. This wedding is to be blessed by the Goddess and God, so that better favor will be shed upon the couple. Perform a full ritual, including cleansing the circle, casting the circle, calling the quadrants, and calling the Goddess and God. The couple needs to have a makeshift altar with all the tools.

Recite the incantation together. The couple reads new words they have written in promise to each other. The rings are blessed with holy water, passed through the flame of one white candle, submerged in earth and finally a white feather is passed through them. The rings are placed on each other's fingers. The couple kisses and will spend the remaining years of marriage blessed by the Goddess and God.

INCANTATION

> *The eclipse of our lives has waned,*
> *We stand for blessings to gain.*
> *Our circle once divided by two,*
> *Now joined together anew.*
> *[Erase the dividing line of the circle]*

Three candles of white with Blessed Be,
Unites our love and holy decree.
Our hearts are bonded with respect,
Love and kindness will reflect.
Bless us God with strength and trust,
Give us foundation and earthly crust.
Bless us Goddess with joy and laughter,
Compassion and guidance before and after.
We offer to you our hearts as one,
Bless our lives by moon and sun.
Handfast together, thankful are we,
This is our will, So Mote It Be.

To Bring About Marriage

Sweet Cherry

TIME   Waxing Friday, to begin on the Venus hour.

TOOLS   One brown candle, Lover's oil, Marriage Mind incense, cherries handpicked from one tree, a picture of you and the person you wish to marry, a gold wedding band (doesn't have to be real gold), stones from the cherries, sugar, and a red mojo.

INSTRUCTIONS   Anoint the candle with Lover's oil. Light the candle and the incense. Pick some cherries from only one tree. As you are picking these cherries, visualize your special someone asking for your hand in marriage. After you have picked about one and a half gallons of cherries, take them home to prepare your brew.

Take the picture of the two of you and roll it up so that you can place the ring around it. Squeeze the juice out of the cherries, but keep the cherrystones and wash them off well. Add sugar to your cherry juice so it's sweet to the taste. Place the cherrystones and the scroll and ring in the red mojo and seal it shut. Recite the incantation over the cherry juice and mojo.

Serve the brew to the person you wish to marry on the Full Moon. Place the mojo in your pillowcase until the day of your wedding. On your wedding day, bury the mojo under a cherry tree.

Incantation

> *Sweet cherry, my love needs quenched,*
> *A proposal of marriage is what I request.*
> *Place the offer upon his bended knee,*
> *With his heart so full when he asks of me.*
> *A life eternal in our wedded bliss,*
> *Sealed forever within our kiss.*
> *My husband's words are within this brew,*
> *Speak them now, I beseech of you.*
> *So Mote It Be.*

TO SOLIDIFY A RELATIONSHIP

Wee Folk Brownies

TIME   Waxing Friday, Venus hour.

TOOLS   One brown candle, Beloved oil, and Handfast incense.

FOR BROWNIES   One cup and two heaping tablespoons of flour, 1/2 cup of Hershey's cocoa, 3/4 cup Nestle's semisweet morsels, two teaspoons of baking soda, 3/4 cup of sugar, one tablespoon of brown sugar, one teaspoon of vanilla, two eggs, 3/4 cup of water, 1/4 cup of applesauce, two tablespoons of vegetable oil, and one teaspoon of cherry extract.

INSTRUCTIONS   Anoint the candle with Beloved oil. Light the candle and the incense.

In a medium-size bowl, mix together all of the dry ingredients (flour through brown sugar). In a large bowl, mix together all of the wet ingredients (vanilla through cherry extract). Recite incantation number one, then combine the dry ingredients with the wet ones. Visualize your lover and you becoming as one as you stir.

Lightly spray a nonstick-baking dish with cooking spray. Bake at 350° Fahrenheit for 20 to 25 minutes.

When the brownies are done, recite incantation number two over the brownies. Cut them into twelve pieces and serve to your lover any time during the next forty-eight hours.

INCANTATION 1

> *Brownies, Faeries, and the Elves,*
> *Grant us love served by twelve.*
> *Tiptoe through my lover's cake,*
> *Bond our love that will not break.*
> *So Mote It Be.*

INCANTATION 2

> *Cupid's arrows and Wee Folk,*
> *Strengthen the love that I invoke.*
> *Sweet and warm our love becomes,*
> *Solid, growing become as one.*
> *Mystic Faeries work in haste,*
> *Love is craving for this taste.*
> *Bless our union and this spell,*
> *All be happy and all be well.*
> *So Mote It Be.*

TO BRING A LOST PET BACK HOME

Golden Retriever

TIME   Any day, Moon hour.

TOOLS   One brown candle, one gold candle, Knock at My Door oil, Come to Me incense, a pinch of catnip, a pinch of chicken bouillon, a bowl of dry food for your pet, a bowl of water, a gold ribbon, a metal wind chime, and a magnet.

INSTRUCTIONS   Anoint both candles with Knock at My Door oil. Light the candles and the incense. Scatter the catnip and chicken bouillon around the edges of the dry pet food. Place the water bowl and food bowl outside the same door the animal left from. Place the gold ribbon at the top of the chime; stick the magnet to the chime as well. Place the chime so it hangs above the food and water. Recite the incantation over the food, water, and chime before you place them in position. The animal should return home within 48 hours.

INCANTATION

> *Precious life that I adore,*
> *Return at once to our door.*
> *Hear the music above the trees,*
> *Hear my call that you must heed.*
> *Home is waiting with your prize,*
> *Place yourself before my eyes.*
> *[Say pet's name twice] I call your name,*
> *Return at once to your domain.*
> *So Mote It Be.*

TO KEEP YOUR MATE AT HOME BY YOUR SIDE

Homeward Bound

TIME   Hare Moon, Venus hour.

TOOLS   One brown candle, one pink candle, Hearth oil, Stay at Home incense, the ingredients for delicious, moist chocolate fudge, two fresh cherries, a CD of Celtic music, and a deck of tarot cards.

INSTRUCTIONS   Anoint the two candles with Hearth oil. Light the candles and the incense. Gather the ingredients to make chocolate fudge. After all of the ingredients have been well mixed add the juice of the two cherries. Eat the skin of the cherries. Recite the incantation. Place the cherry pits on the back porch of your home. Make the fudge to perfection. Play the Celtic music and get out the tarot cards. Ask your mate to stay with you; say that you would like to read his/her cards. Make it fun and enjoyable. Share the fudge with your mate and make sure that he/she takes the first bite. If you take the first bite, the spell will not work. Tell your mate how much you enjoy a night at home together. You may repeat this spell at any time.

INCANTATION

Chocolate candy, cherry spice,
Weave my spell soft and nice.
Make his/her focus just on me,
Laughing, loving, fantasy.
Mesmerized by every card,
Loving me is never hard.
Sharing words and the time,
Never wanting to leave my side.
So Mote It Be.

To Obtain a Spouse or Life-Partner

The Indian Warrior Cry

TIME   Full Moon, Mars hour.

TOOLS   One large brown candle, Handfast oil, Marriage Mind incense, two or three cups of mud, a pinch of lady's mantle, a teaspoon of maidenhair, two pieces of mandrake, a found feather from a crow or any black bird, a piece of pink parchment, a red ink pen, and a corn husk.

INSTRUCTIONS   This was an old Indian spell that worked very well for young Indian maidens seeking their husbands. Anoint the candle with Handfast oil. Light the candle and the incense. With the two cups of mud, create a poppet that resembles the sex of a male or female, depending on which you would like to marry. Place the lady's mantle, maidenhair, and mandrake inside of the poppet. Place the stem of the bird's feather through the heart area of the poppet. Anoint the poppet with the Handfast oil. On the pink parchment, write with the red ink exactly what qualities you would like your mate to have. Burn the parchment by the brown candle's flame. Place the ashes in the burned incense. After all the ashes have cooled, go outside to a cornfield or an outdoor place that you have

Create a mud poppet for this ancient love spell.

chosen to be your altar. Place the ashes upon the bottom of your bare feet. Put your mud poppet into the cornhusk. Recite the incantation. Return to your home and tell no one of your spell. Wait until dawn breaks. The very first dog that you hear barking will tell you to retrieve your mud poppet. If the poppet is gone or broken, the Great Spirit requests that your marriage not take place this year. If the poppet is intact, bury it on the spot, to return it to the earth. Do not come back to this place until after you have been married.

INCANTATION

> *Coyote calling! Thunderstorm!*
> *Spirits passing in darkened sky.*
> *Ashened feet in field of corn,*
> *Brave warrior of midnight cry.*
> *Ebony sparrow stabs his heart,*
> *Carry his love swiftly to me.*
> *My mate, my spouse, forever more,*
> *As green silk protects this seed.*
> *Marriage calls to possess his heart,*
> *With love he calls to his mate.*
> *Dawn will break at the start,*
> *Barking dog now seals our fate.*
> *So Mote It Be.*

TO RETURN HARMONY TO THE HOME AFTER PROBLEMS OR UPHEAVALS

Peaceful Pie

TIME   Waxing Friday, Mercury hour.

TOOLS   Whatever pie crust you make or purchase, one quarter teaspoon of chamomile, one large brown candle, Cedarwood incense, Lavender Blue oil, fresh raspberry pie filling, and one tablespoon of finely ground dulse.

INSTRUCTIONS Prepare the pie crust as your favorite recipe calls for except adding the finely powdered chamomile into the crust. Anoint the brown candle with Lavender Blue oil. Light the candle and the incense. Prepare your raspberry filling with an extra teaspoon of sugar more than your normal taste or what the recipe calls for. Add the dulse to the raspberries. Add the raspberries to the bottom crust. You can add a top crust if you choose. Recite the incantation and suffumigate the whole pie three times deosil over the incense. Place in the oven and bake. Serve to your unsuspecting family by the light of the brown candle.

INCANTATION

Peaceful pie, pie of peace,
Make the darkness still and cease.
Restore the love, restore the laughter,
Happiness abounds us ever after.
Family be healthy, family be whole,
Rebuild the love, it is our goal.
Peaceful pie, pie of peace,
Unleash your magick as we feast.
So Mote It Be.

TO SHIELD YOUR PARTNER FROM A FLIRT

A Witch's Scorn

TIME Full Moon, Mars hour.

TOOLS One brown candle, Frankincense oil, Exorcism incense, a fingerprint of the person who is trying your patience, a pinch of belladonna, and a pinch of mandrake. (One good place to get a usable fingerprint for this spell is from a plastic drinking glass.)

INSTRUCTIONS Anoint the candle with Frankincense oil. Light the candle and the incense. Cut the fingerprint away from the whatever object you used to obtain the fingerprint. Visualize the person who is trying to get at your partner. Sprinkle the belladonna and the mandrake into the brown flame. Keep the visualization of the person and add the fingerprint to the flame. Recite the incantation. After the spell is complete, visualize this person lying in bed dreaming about you. Wake this person with abruptness in your visualization. When next you see this person in the flesh, you must deliver the evil eye. This will effect his or her energy and show that you mean business. Please understand this spell is not based upon hate—but rather it is used to sustain your territorial presence.

INCANTATION

> *From eve of night to break of morn,*
> *Feel the wrath of Witch's scorn.*
> *Back into the sable flame,*
> *To the dream from where you came.*
> *Nightshade sprinkled with Lord of Drake,*
> *For I am the reason that you awake.*
> *Do not tread where Witches dare,*
> *When evil eye says "beware."*
> *So Mote It Be.*

TO HELP STEPSIBLINGS DEVELOP FRIENDSHIP BONDS

Step by Step

TIME   Hare Moon, Mercury hour.

TOOLS   One brown candle for each child, Ravenwood oil, Knock at My Door incense, a yellow piece of parchment, a pink ink pen, and a small brown paper sack.

INSTRUCTIONS   Anoint all of the candles with Ravenwood oil. Light the candles and the incense. Independently, ask each child what he or she likes about the new stepsibling. Write it on the upper portion of the yellow parchment in the pink ink. Each needs to list three things about each other sibling. Ask each what he or she dislikes about the stepsibling, and write it on the lower half of the parchment. Do this with each child without the other children knowing about it. Suffumigate the entire parchment. Then rip the positive half away from the negative half. Recite the incantation. Burn the dislike portion of the parchment by the flame of the brown candle. Place the cooled ashes into the brown bag. Place the positive half of the parchment into the bag also. Add the cooled incense to the bag. Dig a hole north of your home and bury the brown bag. Make sure you drop subtle hints to each of the children as to what "positive" things the other sibling(s) had to say. Within one moon cycle of the spell there will be a huge improvement in the home and the siblings' relationships with each other. This spell can be repeated as often as necessary.

INCANTATION

Step by step,
The spell is cast.
A family bond,
Begins at last.
Words of kindness,
Upon the ear.
Makes each sibling,
Warm and dear.
Love will blossom,
Like a rose.
Extending each petal,
In symmetric pose.
The positive thoughts,
That each has said.
Are securely planted,
North of homestead.
The negative thoughts,
Have burned to ash.

Destroying the issues,
Of a negative past.
Together we bond,
As a family sight.
Happy and loving,
As steps unite.
So Mote It Be.

Sometimes magick is necessary when creating a new family.

To Encourage a Timely Marriage Proposal

The Buried Bouquet

Time   Hare Moon, Venus hour.

Tools   One brown candle, one pink candle, Lover's oil, Marriage Mind incense, the following fresh flowers: orange blossoms, lavender, pink rose, violet, and baby's breath, a twelve-inch brown ribbon, a red ink pen, pink parchment, a rhodonite stone, and a red mojo.

Instructions   Anoint both of the candles with the Lover's oil. Light the candles and the incense. Arrange the fresh flowers in a beautiful bouquet. Tie them together with the brown ribbon. Write your two names in red ink onto the pink parchment. Light the parchment by the flame of the brown candle and burn it to ashes. Recite the incantation. Place the rhodonite stone and the cooled ashes from the parchment into the red mojo. Take two petals from each flower and place into the red mojo. Lightly anoint the mojo with Lover's oil. Give your lover the beautiful bouquet on the next waxing Friday. Keep the mojo well hidden somewhere near him/her, without mentioning its presence. After the proposal has been received, you must bury the red mojo on the first Full Moon that comes, at the midnight hour. Recite the incantation over the burial so as to seal the engagement.

Incantation

> *Marriage flowers, pass him/her not,*
> *Say the words that I have sought.*
> *The moon is half, but when it's whole,*
> *The passions of love will seize your soul.*
> *Bring his/her promise of love to me,*
> *For these words will set you free . . .*

"Will you be my mate,
Marriage is our fate."
The magick potion will do the rest,
Bonding our love is what it does best.
Life together from this point on,
Is as happy and blissful as the day is long.
So Mote It Be.

11

SPELLS THAT ARE

> Return the turn and send it back,
> A Witch reversed the curse attack.
> Gray and pewter will repel
> Slander, hate, and negative spell.
> —Belladonna

The color gray represents magick involving rejection, binding, directing negative energy back to its source, repelling, redirecting, and confusion.

TO COUNTERACT THE EFFECTS OF A NEGATIVE CHAIN LETTER

The Chain Game

TIME   Waning Saturday, Saturn hour. (Even if the chain letter requests an immediate mailing or something bad will happen, keep the letter under a heavy stone outside your home until the appropriate magickal time.)

TOOLS One gray candle, one black candle, JuJu oil, and Widdershins incense. Have the chain letter accessible.

INSTRUCTIONS Anoint both the gray and black candle with JuJu oil. Light the candles and the incense. Retrieve the chain letter. Anoint the letter with the oil in the shape of a releasing pentagram (anoint from the bottom and then draw the pentagram). Pass the letter through the incense smoke and recite the incantation. Dip the bottom corners of the paper in the gray and black candles and let them ignite. Place the burning letter in the cauldron and allow it to burn to ashes. Recite the incantation once again as you release the ashes to the wind.

INCANTATION

> *Papers with threats and malice intent,*
> *I will not submit and I will not consent.*
> *Release the harm that was sent to me,*
> *Or widdershins turn and bring to thee!*
> *So Mote It Be!*

TO REPEL AND KEEP AWAY NEGATIVE ENERGY

The Gray Ghost

TIME Waning Saturday, Saturn hour.

TOOLS One gray candle and Jinx Removing oil.

INSTRUCTIONS Place three drops of Jinx Removing oil in the well of the candle. (The well is where the wick comes out of the candle.) Light the candle and recite the incantation. From that time forward, any time a negative energy is sensed or bad luck is experienced, light the candle and recite the incantation.

INCANTATION

Ghost of gray that whirl about,
Seek the sender of evil and doubt.
Repel and forbid the energy to cross,
My path is winning and never at loss.
So Mote It Be.

To Stop Unwanted Love

The Love Breaker

TIME   Begin this spell on a waning Saturday, Saturn hour.

TOOLS   Five gray candles, Love Breaker oil and incense, a clear jar, Four Thieves vinegar, some of your urine, a hematite, a picture of the man possessed with love, and an apple seed.

INSTRUCTIONS   This spell is to be used only if you have cast a love spell on someone and you find that you no longer want his affections. Anoint the candles with Love Breaker oil. Light the five gray candles and the incense. If you have love letters from this person and no longer want them, place them in the jar along with Four Thieves vinegar and the hematite. Add three drops of your urine to this potion. Visualize this person walking away from you and finding love on a different path. Tape his picture to the jar backwards so that the face of the picture is looking into the jar.

Let this potion steep for ten days during the waning moon. Every day for ten days, light the gray candles and visualize him walking away. On the tenth day, dig a hole away from your home and place the jar in the hole. Place the apple seed in the dirt after you bury the jar. After the jar and the apple seed are buried, recite the incantation. Your ex love will be out of your life within thirty days.

INCANTATION

The well of love has gone dry,
It is not to blame or wonder why.
The juice of thieves must steal you away,
Within this moment and without delay.
The stone of mirrors will wane the desire,
The poison liquid will dowse your fire.
Away you go and out of my life,
No longer are you within my sight.
Your love now empty will never grieve,
For in my stead, is a new love seed.
So Mote It Be.

For a Divorce

The Decree

TIME   Waning Saturday, Saturn hour.

TOOLS   A gray candle, Bending oil, Love Breaker incense, pieces of your spouse's hair, a piece of your spouse's shirt, violets, onion, garlic, black pepper, dirt, and a red mojo.

INSTRUCTIONS   Anoint the gray candle with Bending oil. Light the candle and the incense, and pray to the God for your spouse to want a peaceful divorce. Place pieces of your spouse's hair, a piece of his shirt, violets, onion, garlic, black pepper, and some dirt in the mojo. Do not seal this mojo shut. On a waning Saturday at the Saturn hour, meditate upon the dismissal of your marriage. Then go into a wooded area with your mojo and find the carcass of an animal that has died, like a bird or a mouse. *Be sure you have had no part in this animal's demise.* Read the incantation and act accordingly. Mark a headstone for the creature with the red mojo. Do not come back to this area until the divorce is final.

INCANTATION

> *Take the strand of your spouse's mane,*
> *Violets, onion, garlic, pepper, and terrain.*
> *Place them in the scarlet flannel,*
> *Take them to a deceased animal.*
> *Find a creature that is dead and rotting,*
> *Bury the body if divorce you're plotting.*
> *Sprinkle the remains with the potion,*
> *This will begin the proper motion.*
> *Release the soul from its debt,*
> *Bury with love the nature's pet.*
> *You wish your spouse no harm to come,*
> *The parting of ways, a new life begun.*
> *Say these words as the potion falls,*
> *Goddess and God, upon Thee I call.*
> *No murder has befallen,*
> *This creature nor my mate.*
> *Life was once within us,*
> *Now a change of fate.*
> *A new life for me,*
> *A new life for you.*
> *This creature will live again,*
> *When our lives begin anew.*
> *No longer do we suffer the pain,*
> *Endings come while in the wane.*
> *Saturn help to seal this strife,*
> *Begin a separate, happy life.*
> *The decree is marked upon this grave,*
> *The end of the path is now paved.*
> *So Mote It Be.*

To Return Negativity to Its Source

Backasswards

Time   Waning Saturday, Saturn hour.

Tools   A large gray candle, Rose Cross oil, Widdershins incense, white parchment, gray parchment, Dove's Blood ink, and a freestanding mirror.

Instructions   Anoint the gray candle with Rose Cross oil. Light the candle and the incense. Write the negative words the person said to or about you on white parchment. On the gray parchment with the Dove's Blood ink, write the same words in reverse order ("I hate you" becomes "You hate I").

Place the freestanding mirror behind the incense and the candle so the mirror is facing west and the reflection of the candle and the incense faces west. Write the offending person's name at the bottom of the gray parchment. Anoint both parchments with Rose Cross oil. Using the flame of the gray candle, light the white parchment and then the gray parchment. Recite the incantation. Place the burning parchments in the incense burner and allow them to burn together. The oil makes the parchment burn extremely fast. Anytime you feel the person's negativity near you, relight the gray candle, facing west, with the mirror behind it. This will keep your enemy at bay.

Incantation

> *Said been have words gray,*
> *Sent be will regrets pay.*
> *Flow positive lack that words,*
> *Go to sender, Back-ass-wards.*
> *Be It Mote So.*

To Get Rid of a Horrible Neighbor

Rattle the Snake

TIME   Hare Moon, Moon hour.

TOOLS   One dark gray candle, Rose Cross oil and incense, five cups of water, five tablespoons of sugar, the core of an apple, a blender, a glass container, and a rattlesnake's rattle. (Please remember that we do not harm animals in any way. Please obtain the tail of a rattlesnake that died from natural causes.)

INSTRUCTIONS   Anoint the candle with the Rose Cross oil. Light the candle and the incense. Place five cups of water, the sugar, and the apple core in the blender. Recite the incantation while blending until it is all liquid. Place the contents in a glass container.

When the neighbor is not home, sprinkle the entire mixture around the neighbor's property, carefully making sure that you do not trespass. With the tail of the snake in your power hand, shake the rattle and recite the incantation again.

Every day, light the gray candle and shake the rattle to keep the neighbor at bay. Never let anyone see you do any part of this spell. This spell will encourage the neighbor to move far away from you or at least stay away from you.

INCANTATION

> *With the core and sweetened juice,*
> *I conjure the snake to make a truce.*
> *With every noise that we shall make,*
> *Give this neighbor a shiver and quake.*
> *Upon his/her ground and around his/her feet,*
> *Snakes will slither and soon shall seep.*
> *Into the house and around the one,*

Who causes my pain and whom I shun.
I conjure the snakes upon the path,
To this enemy, feel all of my wrath.
Potion in place and rattle to rattle,
Cease my enemy with whom I battle.
So Mote It Be.

TO DRIVE AWAY SOMEONE WHO WISHES TO STEAL YOUR LOVER

Ant She Charming

TIME   Waning Saturday, Saturn hour.

TOOLS   One gray candle, Love Breaker oil, Spell Breaker incense, an active anthill, a picture of the person who is charming your lover, a silver charm bracelet, one cup of cider vinegar, and one Milk Dud.

INSTRUCTIONS   Anoint the candle with Love Breaker oil. Light the candle and the incense. Place the gray candle in the center of the anthill. Place the picture beneath the gray candle. Place the charm bracelet around the candle. Pour the cider vinegar around the bracelet. Recite the incantation. Place Milk Dud on the face of the picture. Wait thirteen minutes before extinguishing the candle.

After three days, return to the anthill and retrieve the bracelet and the candle. All the other ingredients should remain undisturbed (if there is anything left). The charmer will soon become a dud in the eyes of your lover.

INCANTATION

Little workers of the sand,
Repel all charms and make them banned.
Seduction is the objective key,
Release all charms and make them free.

> *Repel all unconscious attraction,*
> *With this face, make subtraction.*
> *Rebel, repel my lover's desire,*
> *From this person of conspire.*
> *Reverse the charmer with this face,*
> *Trip, stumble, halt the chase.*
> *I offer you this sweet reward,*
> *For releasing my heart's discord.*
> *So Mote It Be.*

To Banish Energy-Stealing Specters and Remove Ghostly Earth Shadows

Dispelling Earth Shadows

TIME   Waning Saturday, Saturn hour.

INGREDIENTS   One white candle, Banishing oil, one gray candle, Criss-Cross oil, Moonlight incense, three cups of purified water, five cups of sea salt, a magickal mirror, and a black cloth.

INSTRUCTIONS   Anoint the white candle with Banishing oil. Anoint the gray candle with Criss-Cross oil. Light the white candle and the incense. Create holy water of consecration by putting two pinches of sea salt into the three cups of water and blessing it. Recite Incantation 1. With the white candle in hand, sprinkle the perimeter of the outside of the house. Do this in deosil motion. Recite Incantation 2 as you do this. Wash the magickal mirror with the consecrated water and recite Incantation 3. Now light the gray candle and carry it outside. Sprinkle the sea salt again, but this time go in widdershins motion. Recite Incantation 4 as you do this. Hang your magickal mirror on the highest level and most western wall of the home. Sprinkle the consecrated water in deosil motion inside the home, starting on the lowest level and working upwards. Finish the ritual in the room where the magickal mirror hangs. Recite Incantation 5 in each and every room of the house. Facing the mirror, recite Incantation 6. Cover the mirror with the black cloth. Leave the mirror covered until all of the earth shadows have disappeared. Then wash the cloth and move the mirror into another room. Normally the earth shadows will be gone within twenty-four hours.

Banish entities from a haunted house.

Incantation 1

Evil be gone,
You have no power.
This home is blessed,
By Angelic Towers.
Raphael, Michael,
Gabriel, and Uriel!
Drive out the evil,
Desist and vanish!
All demons be gone,
Evil be banished!
So Mote It Be.

Incantation 2

Ghosting spirits must now leave,
No more time can you thieve.
Days of wandering are now gone,
Ghostly spirits leave by dawn.
So Mote It Be.

Incantation 3

I close the portal to this mirror,
I close the portal to all my fear.
Doors be doors, locked and keyed,
Never to enter my home or deed.
So Mote It Be.

Incantation 4

Widdershins, widdershins,
Backwards flow.
Widdershins, widdershins,
Out you go!
So Mote It Be.

INCANTATION 5

> *I bless this room with love and light,*
> *Holy Trinities and Angels unite!*
> *So Mote It Be.*

INCANTATION 6

> *Escapement through the Sorcerer's glass,*
> *Free your soul as you pass.*
> *Shrouds of darkness cover and veil,*
> *Portals close as time will fail.*
> *So Mote It Be.*

To Instantly Repel Another

The Bum's Rush

TIME   Waning Tuesday, Mercury hour.

TOOLS   One gray candle, Leopard oil, JuJu incense, a copied photo of the same person, the written name of the person you want to repel, and your urine.

INSTRUCTIONS   Anoint the candle with Leopard oil. Light the candle and the incense. Dig a hole at least thirteen inches deep. Place the photo, face up, into the hole. Place the parchment with the person's name on top of the photo. Then for the big finish, either urinate into the hole or pour your captured urine in the hole. Recite the incantation and fill in the hole. The person will be repelled from you instantly.

INCANTATION

> *Quicken Mars, Quicken Refrain,*
> *Repel this person in this wane.*
> *Flee from me and keep at bay,*
> *Keep your distance far away.*

> *Cast me from your thought and sight,*
> *Your memory fogs in dark of night.*
> *Rushed you be from here to there,*
> *No longer in my glance or stare.*
> *So Mote It Be.*

TO REMOVE OBSTACLES BETWEEN YOU AND YOUR GOAL

Gray Ashbury

TIME   Waning Saturday, Moon hour.

TOOLS   One gray candle, Black Musk oil, Leopard incense, a black ink pen, one piece of gray parchment, a smidgen of benzoin, and one cup of sea salt.

INSTRUCTIONS   Dig a hole near a tree that you will never return to. Anoint the candle with Black Musk oil. Light the candle and the incense. Write upon the gray parchment exactly everything that prohibits you from obtaining your goal. Be very specific about what you need to banish from your life. Anoint the parchment with Black Musk oil. Suffumigate the parchment ten times in widdershins. Place the benzoin in the hole. Ignite the parchment by the gray candle and make sure it is completely burned to ash before you drop it into the hole. Recite the incantation. Fill in the hole using the same dirt. Place the sea salt over the hole. Leave—and never return or look back.

INCANTATION

> *Ashes gray,*
> *Don't stand in my way.*
> *Obstacles be free,*
> *Never surround me.*
> *Goals be near,*
> *I shall not fear.*

Success is mine,
Now is the time.
No more delays,
To successful days.
Beneath this tree,
All obstacles be.
Into the soil,
I banish the toil.
The earth will swallow,
And never will follow.
I shall cheer,
All I hold dear.
There are no binds,
Freedom is mine.
So Mote It Be.

To Divert Another's Passion For You

Passion-Less

Time   Any

Tools   A tossed salad with iceberg lettuce, carrots, and broccoli, one gray candle, Spell Breaker oil, Love Breaker incense, a dash of mentholated rub, and a small amount of hairspray.

Instructions   Prepare a wonderful tossed salad. Top it off with a creamy dressing rather than vinegar and oil. Anoint the candle with Spell Breaker oil. Light the candle and the incense. Visualize a blue-gray aura around yourself. Recite the incantation over the salad. Place a small amount of mentholated rub behind your ears and on your chest. While the person is eating the salad and unknown to him or her, place a small amount of hairspray on your finger and smudge it on his/her third eye. Be as casual as possible when you do this. By the time the salad has been finished, all passions should be diverted, but it will remain so for only twenty-four hours.

INCANTATION

> *Passions stop the ebb and flow,*
> *No desires can forward go.*
> *Third eye close for rest and sleep,*
> *Peaceful wells still and deep.*
> *Energy gone, free will gone,*
> *No physical stress till well past dawn.*
> *Passionless brew now to eat,*
> *Close your eyes for well-deserved sleep.*
> *Head to rest, body to rest,*
> *All the passions now lie west.*
> *Flow this peace from head to toe,*
> *Rest, sleep, desires must go.*
> *So Mote It Be.*

TO PREVENT SLANDER AND STOP NEGATIVE GOSSIP

Dying Words

TIME   Waning Saturday, Saturn hour.

TOOLS   One large gray candle, Obsidian oil, two tablespoons of crushed or powdered cloves, JuJu incense, Dove's Blood ink, nine small pieces of gray parchment, a cauldron, and a copy of Psalm 48.

INSTRUCTIONS   Anoint the candle with Obsidian oil. Place a large pinch of crushed cloves in the JuJu incense. Light the candle and the incense. Write the name of the gossiper on one piece of the gray parchment nine times. Anoint the parchment with Obsidian oil. Burn the parchment and place the burning parchment into the cauldron until it is just ash. Recite the incantation as it burns. Dig a hole that is west of your home and place the ashes into it. Recite

Psalm 48 over the hole. Repeat this spell for nine consecutive days at the Saturn hour and recite the incantation each time. The gossiper will soon lose all interest in talking about you.

INCANTATION

> Ash to Ash,
> Are words that bash.
> Stop the chain,
> That speaks my name.
> As your flame burns,
> Escapement yearns.
> Your words be blind,
> Silence be kind.
> Ash to Ash,
> Your tongue not lash.
> Think me well,
> No lies to tell.
> So Mote It Be.

TO RID A HOME OF EVIL

The Seven-Day Cleansing

TIME   (Make the potion three days prior to casting the spell.) Waning Saturday, Saturn hour.

TOOLS   One teaspoon of red clover, one quart of white distilled vinegar, one large black candle, one white seven-knob wishing candle, Midnight oil, Banishing incense, and three pounds of sea salt.

INSTRUCTIONS   Place the red clover in one quart of distilled vinegar. Let the mixture sit undisturbed in the bottle for three days prior to the waning Saturday. Upon the waning Saturday, Saturn hour, anoint the black candle and the white seven-knob wishing candle with Midnight oil. Light just the black candle and the incense. Make a huge circle of salt around the outside perimeter of the home. Suffumigate the outside of the house in widdershins with the incense. Sprinkle the potion in each room of the house. Recite the incantation as you suffumigate each room, too. Light the white seven-knob candle and place it in the first room that you sprinkle the potion in. Do not leave the house until one knob is completely burned. Extinguish the candles and repeat the next day. Do this for seven consecutive days. Each time a knob is completely burned, leave the house so that no one will disturb your spell. No one should be in the house except for the person casting the spell—and then only during the casting. After the spell is complete, the residents can move back into the home.

INCANTATION

Evil be gone,
You have no power.
This home is blessed,
By Angelic Towers.
Raphael, Michael,
Gabriel, and Uriel!
Drive out the evil,
Desist and vanish!
All demons be gone,
Evil be banished!
So Mote It Be.

12

SPELLS THAT ARE *Black*

> A Witch will burn the midnight oil,
> When legal papers suffer and spoil.
> Avert the wrath of the angry judge,
> With sage and gavel, smoke and smudge.
> —Belladonna

The color black represents magick involving banishment, removal of negative influences, secrecy, legal manipulation, and destruction of harmful energy.

TO PUT AN END TO A LAWSUIT

A Cold Day in Hell

TIME   Waning Saturday, Saturn hour.

TOOLS   One black candle, Saturn oil, Black Candle Tobacco incense, one red bell pepper, ginger, and tobacco.

INSTRUCTIONS   Generously anoint the candle with Saturn oil. Light the candle and the incense. Visualize the candle as a sword. You will visualize yourself cutting through the legal papers and igniting them with this candle. Also imagine your enemy's face when you win. Ask for the help of the God to give you an easy victory over your opponent.

Slice the red bell pepper in half. Place ginger and tobacco inside the pepper. Run water over the pepper. Then place Saturn oil inside the pepper. Place the pepper and the lit black candle into the freezer (it will go out as soon as you shut the door). Recite the incantation. Do not remove the pepper or disturb it until all court battles have ceased. When all feels safe, completely burn the red bell pepper and scatter the remains in water.

INCANTATION

> *Enemy has search and found my path,*
> *Judgment comes for the God has wrath.*
> *Blackened flame burn and swell,*
> *Extinguish my enemy like cold in hell.*
> *End all ends by conquering these foes,*
> *Their power is drained and now is froze.*
> *The sword has fallen and the fire wanes,*
> *Victory is now mine to claim.*
> *So Mote It Be.*

TO BIND A NEGATIVE ENERGY FOREVER

The Coffin

TIME   Waning Moon, any hour.

TOOLS   A black candle, Repelling oil, Bind and Drive incense, a small mirror, a small cardboard box that is not square, bella donna, devil's shoestring, mandrake, and black electrical tape.

INSTRUCTIONS   Anoint the candle with Repelling oil. Light the candle and the incense. Glue the small mirror to the inside of the cardboard lid. Put the herbs in the box. If there are any photographs, letters, or anything that has inspired this negative energy, burn them and place the ashes into the box. Seal the box with the electrical tape so it will never be opened. It is best to cover the box completely with the tape. Bury the box away from your home. Recite the incantation over the burial.

INCANTATION

> *Blackened box and eternal coffin,*
> *Never to open, never escape.*
> *Bound within darkness often,*
> *Never to open, never escape.*
> *Sighted with only ebony dreams,*
> *Never to open, never escape.*
> *Reflecting only hellish schemes,*
> *Never to open, never escape.*
> *Casted down into earthly soil,*
> *Never to open, never escape.*
> *Bound to destroy evil and toil,*
> *Never to open, never escape.*
> *So Mote It Be.*

TO GAIN FAVOR WITH A JURY OR JUDGE DURING A TRIAL

Grains for Gains

TIME   Waxing Sunday, Jupiter hour.

TOOLS   One purple candle, Bending oil, Snake incense, a Bible, three grains of paradise, and a red mojo.

INSTRUCTIONS   Anoint the candle with Bending oil. Light the candle and the incense. Pray to the Goddess and God that the judge and jury will have complete confidence in you and will find in your favor. Then read Psalm Twenty and Psalm Seventy-Six over the grains of paradise. Place the grains inside the mojo and pass it deosil through the incense smoke. Recite the incantation. Carry the mojo with you to court.

Incantation

> Words of prayer from holy book,
> Encompass sympathy about my look.
> Judge and jury find my favor,
> Win me now and without waiver.
> Bending oil and smoke of snake,
> Paradise grain of three I take.
> Guide me through and without sin,
> Give to me the mighty win.
> So Mote It Be.

To End Your Poverty

Dead Man's Purse

Time Waning Saturday, Saturn hour.

Tools One black candle, Obsidian oil, Black Musk incense, green parchment, a pen with black ink, the coin purse or wallet of a deceased person (it works best if the person has been dead for over a year), a pair of scissors, one piece of mandrake, three coffin nails, and a piece of driftwood.

Instructions Anoint the candle with Obsidian oil. Light the candle and the incense. Upon the green parchment in black ink write "ENOG EB YTREVOP." Cut the parchment in half with the scissors and place both of the pieces in the purse along with the mandrake. Hammer the three coffin nails through the purse into the driftwood. Recite the incantation. Bury the wood into the earth near a cemetery. The poverty will end by the full moon.

Incantation

Upon the wood that drifts by night,
Release the plagues that sting and bite.
Poverty washed upon my shore,
Take it now forevermore.
Upon the wood is nailed a purse,
Dead man watching release the curse.
Within the folds a parchment green,
Cut in half by guillotine.
Beside it lies the Drake of Man,
Forever banished beneath the land.
I give to earth a drowning woe,
Return to me a positive flow.
Dead man's purse and coffin nails,
Thrice be driven without fail.
Break the curse and even the toll,
Bring me money when the moon is whole.
So Mote It Be.

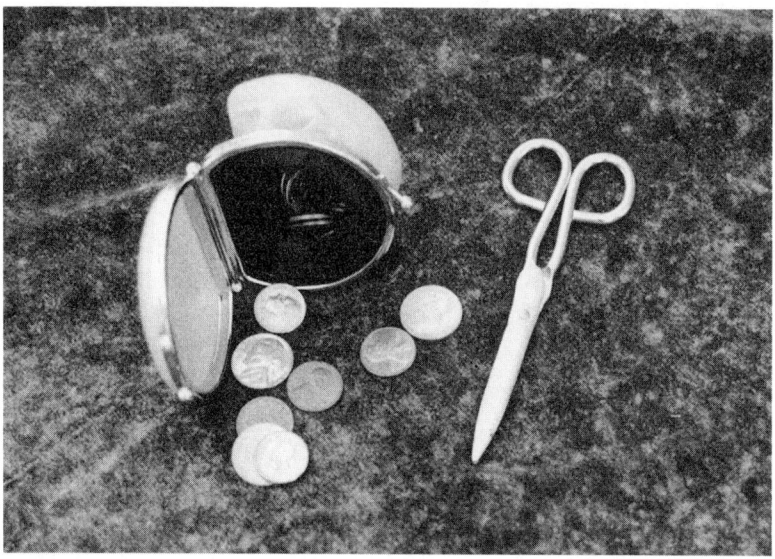

A deceased person's wallet or purse

To End an Intense Bad-Luck Streak

The Egg and I

TIME   Waning Saturday, Mars hour.

TOOLS   One black candle, Banishing oil, Sage incense, one egg, one black cloth, two stickpins with white pearl heads (like old-fashioned hatpins), one cup of cemetery dirt, and about three ounces of consecrated holy water in a paper cup.

INSTRUCTIONS   Anoint the candle with the oil. Light the candle and the incense. Hold the egg in your hands and recite incantation number one. Roll the egg up in the black cloth. Place one pin in each end of the egg, through the black cloth, without cracking the egg. Recite incantation number two. Bury the egg in a deserted area away from your home and cover it with the cemetery dirt. Place the holy water in the paper cup directly on top of the buried egg and leave it there. Recite incantation number three. Stay away from this place for a minimum of one year.

INCANTATION 1

> *Bad luck shift from me to thee,*
> *Cleanse me white, set me free.*
> *So Mote It Be.*

INCANTATION 2

> *Pole to pole, bad luck contained,*
> *Within the egg it now remains.*
> *Mummied in the jacket black,*
> *Defused the energy of attack.*
> *So Mote It Be.*

INCANTATION 3

> *Beneath the earth I bury thee,*
> *No more harm to come to me.*

Spells That Are Black

Soil of death confines the plot,
Destroying the curse as it rots.
I consecrate this mortal ground,
With this water it is bound.
Poison diminish with decay,
All bad luck now go away.
So Mote It Be.

Two straight pins and an egg

To Banish Someone's Obsession With You

Niagara Falls

TIME   Full Moon, Moon hour.

TOOLS   One black candle, Black Musk oil, Widdershins incense, six inches of black material, a small piece of black licorice candy, a crow's feather, a stapler with at least thirteen staples in it, Niagara spray starch, and an iron.

INSTRUCTIONS   After this spell has been cast, there can be no contact of any kind with this person. Anoint the candle with Black Musk oil. Light the candle and the incense. Pass the black cloth widdershins through the incense smoke six times. Place the black cloth on your altar and visualize your life without this person. See yourself happy. Place the black licorice and crow's feather in the cloth and fold the cloth in half. With the stapler, place thirteen staples in the cloth. The staples will hold the sides shut as in making a pocket with no opening. Spray the black pocket with a heavy dose of Niagara spray starch. With a hot iron, iron the pocket and melt the licorice to the feather. Iron it well and make it stiff. Recite the incantation while ironing. When it is done, take the pocket to a deserted field far from you and place beneath a very heavy rock. Do not have any contact with this person whatsoever. Any contact will make *Niagara fall* back into obsession.

INCANTATION

> *Luna, Luna, white and round,*
> *Obsession looked, obsession found.*
> *Release all thoughts he/she has of me,*
> *Banish him/her with your lunacy.*
> *Licorice black,*
> *Cease attack!*
> *Feather of crow,*
> *Make him/her go!*

*Forever melded to ebony,
To yourself instead of me.
Away from me, obsession banished,
Beneath the stone it will vanish.
So Mote It Be.*

To Banish Nightmares

The Night Gallery

Time   Any day or night before you sleep, Saturn hour.

Tools   One black candle, Leopard oil, one blue candle, Astral Projection oil, JuJu incense, a picture of an eagle, and pictures of everyone you love.

Instructions   Anoint the black candle with Leopard oil. Anoint the blue candle with Astral Projection oil. Light the candles and the incense. Turn the head of your bed to the opposite direction it was before. Swirl the eagle's picture widdershins three times around the black candle and swirl it deosil three times around the blue candle. Place the photos on the north wall of your bedroom, like a gallery. Look at your loved ones' photos one by one. Touch their faces and feel their love. Recite the incantation right before you close your eyes to sleep.

Incantation

*Kyrie, Kyrie, eagle's nest,
Protect me from frightful rest.
Love extends from the north,
Dreams be blessed this day forth.
Rise above this earthly plane,
Safely where the Goddess reigns.
Wrap me in her velvet arms,
Forever banned from the harm.
So Mote It Be.*

To End Hatred Between Two People

Ironweed

TIME   Hare Moon, Mars hour.

TOOLS   One pink candle, Forgiveness oil, Friendship incense, two teaspoons of ironweed herb, and one bottle of Southern Comfort.

INSTRUCTIONS   Anoint the candle with Forgiveness oil. Light the candle and the incense. Place the ironweed into the bottle of Southern Comfort. Recite the incantation. Cap the bottle securely and allow to stand in total darkness, undisturbed, for exactly seven days. Strain out the ironweed and recap the bottle. Serve the potion to

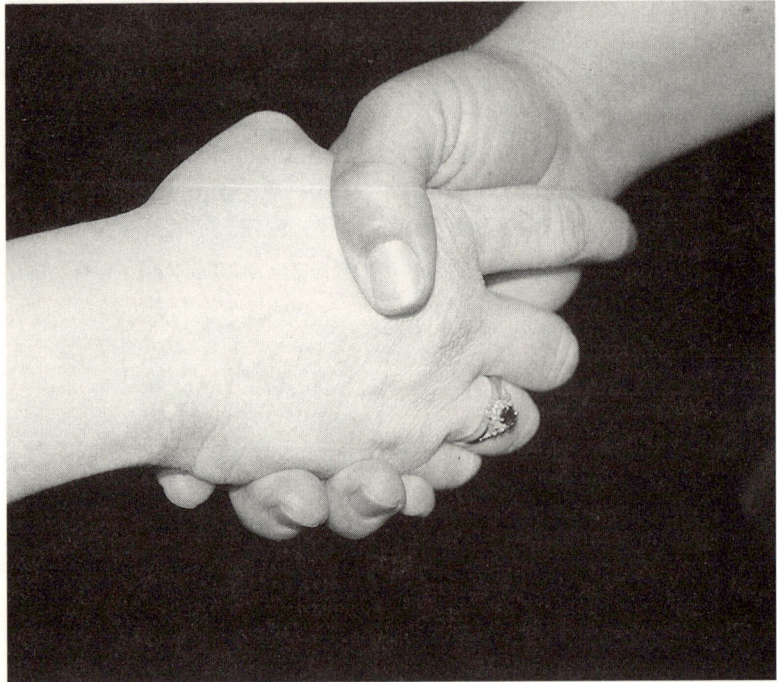

Bitter enemies can become friends.

each of the two people on a Waxing Sunday. Do not serve it to them together, but just on the same day. The bitterness will soon dissipate and finally dissolve. Tell neither of the two people of your meddling spell, or their battle will turn into a war.

INCANTATION

> *Spirit within the ironweed,*
> *Dissolve the hatred, bitterness, and greed.*
> *End the dispute between these two,*
> *Kindness, friendship within this brew.*
> *Stalemate gone, gentleness stay,*
> *Past be past, beginning today.*
> *No longer harbor ill will or pain,*
> *Grant their friendship with loving gain.*
> *So Mote It Be.*

TO WIN THE FAVOR OF THE COURT OR A JURY

The Power of Psalms

TIME   Ten days before your court date, Mercury hour.

TOOLS   One black candle, one gold candle, Ambergris oil, Black Candle Tobacco incense, one teaspoon of galangal, one teaspoon of calendula, one teaspoon of cascara sagrada, a white handkerchief, and a copy of Psalm 7.

INSTRUCTIONS   Anoint both candles with Ambergris oil. Light the black candle and the incense every day at the Mercury hour, for nine days prior to the court date. Add three drops of the oil to the herbs. Place the three herbs in the white handkerchief. Leave the handkerchief undisturbed beneath the mattress of your bed. Recite Psalm 7 out loud each time when you light the black candle for the ritual. On the tenth day, which would be the court date, light the gold candle. Place the handkerchief in front of the gold candle and recite Psalm 7 out loud. Burn the handkerchief to ashes and bury it before you leave for court. Recite the incantation one final time after you bury the ashes.

INCANTATION

> *Psalm of Seven,*
> *Three times three.*
> *Powers of Heaven,*
> *Grant me serenity.*
> *I ask to win,*
> *My day in court.*
> *Today begins,*
> *A total support.*
> *So Mote It Be.*

TO OVERCOME GUILT AND FORGIVE YOURSELF

Divorcing Attitudes

TIME   Waning Tuesday, Sun hour.

TOOLS   One black candle, Leopard oil, New Life incense, white parchment, black ink, something to dig a shallow grave with, two willow branches that are placed in the shape of a cross, and one red rose.

INSTRUCTIONS   Anoint the candle with Leopard oil. Light the candle and the incense. Write the word DIVORCE, across the top of the white parchment with the black ink. On the left side of the paper, write down what has made you feel guilty. On the right side of the paper, write something you have done that you are proud of. Write the incantation on the bottom of the paper. Recite the incantation. Dig a hole six inches deep. Place the "divorce paper," in the hole. Drip wax from the black candle onto the paper. Fill in the hole and bury the paper. Place the willow branches to mark the burial of your guilt. Place the red rose over the cross and promise yourself to never repeat the same mistake that caused you to feel the guilt.

INCANTATION

> *Blackened guilt that once was plague,*
> *Disease be gone, banished and vague.*
> *I now divorce and cast aside,*
> *All the shame that I have cried.*
> *I embrace all that I have lost,*
> *Shame no longer pays that cost.*
> *Leopard's spots smoke and leave,*
> *Here I bury the guilt I've grieved.*
> *So Mote It Be.*

TO DISMISS BINDS, KNOWN OR UNKNOWN, THAT PEOPLE HAVE PUT ON YOU

Blind Binds

TIME   Full Moon, Noon.

TOOLS   One black candle, Black Musk incense, Banishing oil, a magnifying glass, twelve inches of black yarn, and half a cup of red wine vinegar.

INSTRUCTIONS   This spell releases guilt and conditional love. Anoint the candle with the oil. Light the candle and the incense. You need to be outside and the sunlight needs to be strong. It can be very dangerous to play with a magnifying glass to set things on fire, but that's exactly what you need to do. (Evaluate your surroundings to avoid any potential hazards, especially flammable materials.) You need to recite the incantation. Carefully use the magnifying glass to set only one end of the black yarn on fire. As the end is burning, recite the incantation again. While it is still burning, place the yarn into the red wine vinegar. Be very careful not to set anything else on fire, such as your sleeve. (Don't laugh, I've done it.) Bury the yarn and the red wine vinegar near a stream or body of water that is moving away from you. There will be no binds upon you, unless you permit them.

INCANTATION

> *Puppet strings that tug and drag,*
> *Burn away the binds and gag.*
> *Free me from the puppeteer,*
> *Insecurity and the fear.*
> *Remove all guilt and wayward hold,*
> *That made me feel weak and cold.*
> *Set me free with blazing fire,*
> *I will be as I desire.*
> *So Mote It Be.*

TO MAKE A NEGATIVE PERSON LEAVE YOUR NEIGHBORHOOD

Evil Deeds

TIME   Full Moon, Mars hour.

TOOLS   One black candle, a white candle for each household on your block, Dragon's Fire oil, Drive Away Evil incense, thirteen inches of thick, black rope or jute string, a picture of the person you would like to remove from your neighborhood, a hammer, and thirteen coffin nails.

INSTRUCTIONS   Please employ your best judgment when using this spell. A negative person is not just a grumpy person with a bad attitude but is someone seriously bad, who harms children, animals, etc. Take all of the ingredients to the west side of your home. Anoint all of the candles with Dragon's Fire oil. Arrange the white candles in the way that the neighborhood is arranged, using the black candle to represent the negative person. Light the candles and the incense. Suffumigate the black rope in the incense. Tie thirteen knots in the rope and place the person's picture at the bottom of the rope. Starting with the first knot, hammer a coffin nail through the knot. Place a coffin nail in each of the remaining twelve knots. Attach this rope to the west side of your home. Recite the incantation every day until the negative person has moved. After the person has left, burn the rope and the picture. Place the ashes on the vacated property.

INCANTATION

> *Thirteen knots nailed west oppose,*
> *White be friends, black be foes.*
> *Remove the one with evil deed,*
> *Quake the ground and home with speed.*
> *Drive them out with coffin spikes,*
> *Poke and prod them with dislike.*
> *Force them to a distant place,*
> *Remove the foes and friends replace.*
> *So Mote It Be.*

APPENDIX A

THE SORCERESS'S SOURCES

There are two ways to get your magickal supplies. One way, of course, is to make them yourself. You can get instructions on how to make a lot of the incenses and oils in Scott Cunningham's books *The Magick of Incense, Oils and Brews* and *Magickal Herbalism*. Other great books are *Wylundt's Book of Incenses* and *Charms, Spells and Formulas,* by Ray L. Malbrough.

The other way of getting supplies is through a well-stocked occult store. The one that I love is Energy Medicine Arts. This is the place to go for ingredients like Four Thieves powder, Lovely oil, and the other ingredients these spells call for. They have every single incense, oil, and bath salt you can imagine. They have red flannel mojos, magickal stones, a wide range of athames, crystals, music, books, capes, pentagrams, and everything a Witch's heart could ever desire. A truly orgasmic experience for the shopping Sorceress. The address for Energy Medicine Arts is 619 S. College Ave #1, Ft. Collins, Co. 80524. Phone: 970-472-2382. They also have a Web site so you can order over the Internet: www.energymedicinearts.com.

APPENDIX B

TABLE OF MAGICKAL HOURS OF THE DAY

HOURS A.M.	SUN.	MON.	TUES.	WED.	THURS.	FRI.	SAT.
1:00	Sun	Moon	Mars	Merc.	Jup.	Ven.	Sat.
2:00	Ven.	Sat.	Sun	Moon	Mars	Merc.	Jup.
3:00	Merc.	Jup.	Ven.	Sat.	Sun	Moon	Mars
4:00	Moon	Mars	Merc.	Jup.	Ven.	Sat.	Sun
5:00	Sat.	Sun	Moon	Mars	Merc.	Jup.	Ven.
6:00	Jup.	Ven.	Sat.	Sun	Moon	Mars	Merc.
7:00	Mars	Merc.	Jup.	Ven.	Sat.	Sun	Moon
8:00	Sun	Moon	Mars	Merc.	Jup.	Ven.	Sat.
9:00	Ven.	Sat.	Sun	Moon	Mars	Merc.	Jup.
10:00	Merc.	Jup.	Ven.	Sat.	Sun	Moon	Mars
11:00	Moon	Mars	Merc.	Jup.	Ven.	Sat.	Sun
12:00	Sat.	Sun	Moon	Mars	Merc.	Jup.	Ven.

APPENDIX C

TABLE OF MAGICKAL HOURS OF THE NIGHT

HOURS A.M.	SUN.	MON.	TUES.	WED.	THURS.	FRI.	SAT.
1:00	Jup.	Ven.	Sat.	Sun	Moon	Mars	Merc.
2:00	Mars	Merc.	Jup.	Ven.	Sat.	Sun	Moon
3:00	Sun	Moon	Mars	Merc.	Jup.	Ven.	Sat.
4:00	Ven.	Sat.	Sun	Moon	Mars	Merc.	Jup.
5:00	Merc.	Jup.	Ven.	Sat.	Sun	Moon	Mars
6:00	Moon	Mars	Merc.	Jup.	Ven.	Sat.	Sun
7:00	Sat.	Sun	Moon	Mars	Merc.	Jup.	Ven.
8:00	Jup.	Ven.	Sat.	Sun	Moon	Mars	Merc.
9:00	Mars	Merc.	Jup.	Ven.	Sat.	Sun	Moon
10:00	Sun	Moon	Mars	Merc.	Jup.	Ven.	Sat.
11:00	Ven.	Sat.	Sun	Moon	Mars	Merc.	Jup.
12:00	Merc.	Jup.	Ven.	Sat.	Sun	Moon	Mars

ABOUT THE AUTHOR

Sister Moon, who is also the author of *The Wiccaning,* was initiated into the Craft by her grandmother. She lives in Colorado and can be contacted by mail at P.O. Box 2995, Loveland, CO 80538 or by e-mail at sismoon0101@aol.com.